Other Books and Materials
by Pauline Adongo

Victorious Overcomer-Declarations and Prayers for Spiritual Warfare-Manual:
Prayers to break demonic covenants, rituals, dedications, thrones, witchcraft, and altars

(Available in Spanish)- *(Vencedor Victorioso -Declaraciones y oraciones para la guerra espíritu.* Oraciones para romper pactos demoniacos, convenios, dedicaciones, rituales, altares, tronos, maldiciones y brujería.

The Alternative Plan
Pauline's testimony of how God restored her life to align with His intended Plan

Called to Ministry Now What
How to recognize your calling, what to do and how to navigate your encounters with God

Ministry Beyond the Pulpit
Not everyone is called to the platform.
How to use your gifts to influence where God has placed you

Prayer is Simply Talking to God
Everyone can pray effectively; simple steps to jump start your prayer life and receive answers. Prayer is a two-way communication with God

Prayer is Simply Talking to God
CD-Teaching- downloadable versions available on iTunes, CD-Baby and Amazon

Familiarity
Ways in which we can miss God based on an attitude of familiarity
How satan deceives through familiarity

Dreams and Encounter Journal
A journal with instructions of how to follow through on dreams and encounters

Please visit www.paulineadongo.com to purchase these materials
E-book versions of the books are also available

PRAYING THE NAMES
AND
ATTRIBUTES OF GOD

SYNERGY WITH THE TRINITY IN PRAYER
A COLLABORATION WITH EXTRAORDINARY OUTCOMES

PAULINE ADONGO

WESTBOW
PRESS®
A DIVISION OF THOMAS NELSON
& ZONDERVAN

WestBow Press books may be ordered through booksellers or by contacting:

WestBow Press
A Division of Thomas Nelson & Zondervan
1663 Liberty Drive
Bloomington, IN 47403
www.westbowpress.com
1 (866) 928-1240

Requests for bulk sales discounts, editorial permissions, or other information should be addressed to:

The Ministry of Jesus Christ International Inc-MJC
Post Office Box 2572,
West Chester, PA 19380, USA

www.paulineadongo.com
Harvest-Equip-Disciple and Ignite Nations

ISBN: 978-1-9736-9563-9 (sc)
ISBN: 978-1-9736-9562-2 (e)

Print information available on the last page.

WestBow Press rev. date: 07/01/2020

CONTENTS

Dedication..ix

Worship!..xiii

Introduction... xv

Chapter 1   Jeremiah's Prayer-Synergy With God............................ 1
Chapter 2   God My Father 4
Chapter 3   God Who Loves Me 9
Chapter 4   The Holy God.. 13
Chapter 5   God The I Am I Am Who I Am....................................18
Chapter 6   The Almighty God All Powerful God Jehovah El
             Shaddai Omnipotent God 22
Chapter 7   The Lord - Yahweh Jehovah Adonai 27
Chapter 8   The Omniscient The All-Knowing God.........................31
Chapter 9   God My Provider Jehovah Jireh 35
Chapter 10   God My Peace Jehovah Shalom 39
Chapter 11   God My Defense Jehovah Sabaoth Commander
             of the Armies of the Lord.. 43
Chapter 12   God My Banner Jehovah Nissi 48
Chapter 13   The Lord of Justice, Righteouness and Truth.............. 52
Chapter 14   The Lord My Deliverer 56
Chapter 15   The Lord My Shepherd Jehovah Roi............................ 60
Chapter 16   God My Righteouness Jehovah Tsidkenu..................... 65
Chapter 17   God My Sanctifier Jehovah M'kaddesh 68
Chapter 18   The Lord Is There Jehovah Shammah
             The Omnipresent God... 72

Chapter 19 God My Healer Jehovah Rapha Yahweh Rofe'ekha...... 76
Chapter 20 The Lord Who has the Keys to Open and to Shut 81
Chapter 21 The Alpha And Omega The God Of Perfect Timing... 84
Chapter 22 The God Who Remembers... 89
Chapter 23 The God Who Sees 94
Chapter 24 All Consuming Fire... 98
Chapter 25 The Ancient Of Days..103
Chapter 26 The Good God Whose Mercy Endures Forever..........107
Chapter 27 The Lord Restores 111
Chapter 28 The Ominiscient, Omnipresent, Omnipotent God 115
Chapter 29 Names and Attributes of Jesus Christ 119
Chapter 30 Attributes of the Holy Spirit.......................................125
Chapter 31 Benefits of Praying in Tongues 132

The Prayer Of Salvation And The Baptism Of The Holy Spirit 137
About The Author 139

DEDICATION

I am dedicating this book to my little brother Joseph. Jose, this book was written during my short stay with you and the family in the winter of 2020. Thank you for the hospitality you extended by ensuring that all of my amenities, including gym membership, were accommodated. I appreciated the one-on-one conversations, the laughter, your regular visits, and, of course, the food. God brought you into the family as a mediator, one who is able to bring things into perspective. You have a great gift of understanding the unique personalities of each of your siblings, and you have a way blending us together in harmony. You have a genuine love for each of us, you exemplify the true heart of God towards us- this is true of your character as a person. May this book enrich you as well. I love you and will be praying for you.

Blessings and love always.

Polly

The Lord is near to all who call on Him, to all who call
on Him in truth. He fulfills the desires of those who
fear Him; He hears their cry and saves them.
(¹Psalm 145:18,19, ESV)

¹ Scripture quotations identified throughout this book in KJV (King James
Version), NKJV (New King James Versions), NLT (New Living Translation
Version), AMPC(Amplified Version Classic Edition), ESV(English Standard Version),
NIV(New International Version), and NASB (New American Standard Bible) and
others indicated are from www.biblegateway.com

WORSHIP!

Then I looked, and I heard the voice of many angels around the throne, the living creatures, and the elders; and the number of them was ten thousand times ten thousand, and thousands of thousands, saying with a loud voice:

> "Worthy is the Lamb who was slain
> To receive power and riches and wisdom,
> And strength and honor and glory and blessing!"

And every creature which is in heaven and on the earth and under the earth and such as are in the sea, and all that are in them, I heard saying:

> Blessing and honor and glory and power
> *Be* to Him who sits on the throne,
> And to the Lamb, forever and ever!"

Then the four living creatures said, "Amen!" And the twenty-four elders fell down and worshiped Him who lives forever and ever. (Revelation 5:11-14, NKJV)

After these things I looked, and behold, a great multitude which no one could number, of all nations, tribes, peoples, and tongues, standing before the throne and before the Lamb, clothed with white robes, with palm branches in their hands, and crying out with a loud voice, saying, "Salvation belongs to our God who sits on the throne, and to the Lamb!" All the angels stood around the throne and the elders and the four living creatures and fell on their faces before the throne and worshiped God, saying:

> Amen! Blessing and glory and wisdom,
> Thanksgiving and honor and power and might,
> be to our God forever and ever. Amen. ([2]Revelation 7: 9-12,
> NKJV

---

[2] Scripture quotations identified throughout this book in KJV (King James Version), NKJV (New King James Versions), NLT (New Living Translation Version), AMPC(Amplified Version Classic Edition), ESV(English Standard Version), NIV(New International Version), and NASB (New American Standard Bible) and others indicated are from www.biblegateway.com

INTRODUCTION

As I read the Bible I am always captivated by the names and attributes of God. I am often drawn to the origin and application of that Name, and in the context of what is being relayed in the Scriptures. For example, Gideon must have been anxious about his assignment and needed peace, so he encountered the God of peace (see Judges 6:24; NJKV). Abraham was about to offer his only son Isaac as a burnt offering when Isaac asked his father where the lamb was for the sacrifice. Abraham responded, "the Lord will provide; (³Genesis 22:14, NKJV)." Here the Lord did not just provide Abraham a lamb for the immediate sacrifice, but He also gave us a prophesy of the Sacrificial Lamb, Jesus Christ, who would later provide for our redemption (see Genesis 22, NKJV). And there is David, a humble shepherd, who later became a king, who repeatedly spoke of the Great Shepherd in the Psalms.

As I continue to walk with God, I have learned the importance and the power of using Scripture to pray. Through experience with the Holy Spirit in prayer or intercession, the Holy Spirit has led me to use the names and attributes of God as they pertain to the issue I am praying for. This normally leads to an easy transition in the spheres of prayer and much faster breakthroughs as well. I believe this happens because God never changes in His character; He is the One Who Was, Is, and

---

³ Scripture quotations identified throughout this book in KJV (King James Version), NKJV (New King James Versions), NLT (New Living Translation Version), AMPC(Amplified Version Classic Edition),AMP, (Amplified Bible), ESV(English Standard Version), NIV(New International Version), and NASB (New American Standard Bible) and others indicated are from www.biblegateway.com

Is to Come. God cannot recant what He has already said. God stands by His word and watches over it to perform it. God's Word is final and established (see Revelation 1:8, Malachi 3:6, Jeremiah1:12, Isaiah 40:8, Isaiah 55:10-11 and [4]Matthew 24:35 all in NKJV).

I believe that by faith, when we use the Word of God, when we mention His names and attributes in prayer, praise, or petitions - He responds, and meets us where we are. He responds because we have come into agreement with Him, His nature, and His word; we have aligned ourselves with Him and His purposes concerning us. We are engaging His authority and power with the authority and power He has given us. Coming into agreement brings us into synergy with God. *Synergy is the combined power of a group of things when they are working together that is greater than the total power achieved by each working separately([5]dictionary.cambridge.org). Another definition defines [6]synergy as the interaction or cooperation of two or more organizations, substances, or other agents to produce a combined effect greater than the sum of their separate effects.* The Synergy of praying the name and attributes of God brings the reality of these attributes to our natural world and to the issues we are praying for.

While in a season of seeking God through prayer, I sensed that I should use the names and attributes of God as I prayed. I had mostly used them in worship and in prayers of petition. Ten months prior to this I had started studying the names of God as stated in the book of Revelation; but as I was praying, I recalled that I had done the same thing the previous year. Repeated inclinations often mean pay attention, and act on what the Holy Spirit is saying. So, I have written this book from an

---

[4] Scripture quotations identified throughout this book in KJV (King James Version), NKJV (New King James Versions), NLT (New Living Translation Version), AMPC(Amplified Version Classic Edition),AMP, (Amplified Bible), ESV(English Standard Version), NIV(New International Version), and NASB (New American Standard Bible) and others indicated are from www.biblegateway.com

[5] Definition of Synergy www. dictionary. Cambridge.com

[6] https://www.lexico.com/definition/synergy

experiential perspective. As I am learning the meanings of the names of God, I am actively applying them in prayer. Jeremiah's prayer in the next chapter is an example of coming into agreement with God. May your prayer life be enhanced as you come into synergy with God.

In this book, each of God's names and attributes has a short excerpt of Scripture application that you can use and practically apply in prayer, and later use as a declaration for the issue you are praying for. God's names and attributes address every area of life. That is why God is the Great I AM. He is the all-inclusive answer to your specific areas of need, needs that are addressed in this book. May God respond with swift answers to your prayers as you acknowledge His majesty.

The Lord is near to all who call on Him, to all who call on Him in truth. He fulfills the desires of those who fear Him; He hears their cry and saves them (Psalm 145:18-19; NKJV).

Surely the arm of the Lord is not too short to save, nor his ear too dull to hear ([7]Isaiah 59:1; NIV).

---

[7] Scripture quotations identified throughout this book in KJV (King James Version), NKJV (New King James Versions), NLT (New Living Translation Version), AMPC(Amplified Version Classic Edition), ESV(English Standard Version), NIV(New International Version), and NASB (New American Standard Bible) and others indicated are from www.biblegateway.com

JEREMIAH'S PRAYER-SYNERGY WITH GOD

Prayer is a dialogue between the person praying and God. Prayer is a two-way communication that requires waiting to receive God's response when we pray. The above Scriptures are a perfect example of dialogue between God and the Prophet Jeremiah. We, too, should engage with God by faith at this level knowing that God listens and likes to respond to our requests.

*Jeremiah 32: 16- 22-Now when I had delivered the purchase deed to Baruch son of Neriah, **I prayed to the Lord, saying: Alas, Lord God!** Behold, You have made the heavens and the earth by Your great power and by Your outstretched arm! **There is nothing too hard or too wonderful for You-** You Who show loving-kindness to thousands but recompense the iniquity of the fathers into the bosoms of their children after them. The great, the mighty God; the Lord of hosts is His name—Great are You in counsel and mighty in deeds, whose eyes are open to all the ways of the sons of men, to reward or repay each one according to his ways and according to the fruit of his doings. Who wrought signs and wonders in the land of Egypt, **and even to this day continues to do so**, both in Israel and among other men, and made for Yourself a name, as at this day? And You brought forth Your people Israel out of the land of Egypt with signs and wonders, with a strong hand and outstretched arm and with* *great terror; and You gave them this land which You swore to their fathers to give them, a land flowing with milk and honey (AMPC).*

Jeremiah 32: 26-27- Then came the word of the Lord to Jeremiah, saying, **Behold, I am the Lord, the God of all flesh; is there anything too hard for Me?** *(AMPC).*

Scripture Application

Throughout the Bible, God was often addressed by His attributes and abilities; this is evident in both the Old and New Testaments. I am often encouraged by the descriptive attributes of God in the epistles. Such as: "Now to Him who is able to do immeasurably more than all we ask or imagine, according to his power that is at work within us" (Ephesians 3:20; NIV); "To Him who is able to keep you from stumbling and to present you before His glorious presence without fault and with great joy-- to the only God our Savior be glory, majesty, dominion, and authority, through Jesus Christ our Lord, before all time, and now, and for all eternity. Amen" (Jude 1:24-25; NIV); "Now unto the King eternal, immortal, invisible, the only wise God, be honor and glory for ever and ever. Amen" (1 Timothy 1:17; KJV); and the list goes on! These descriptions are affirmations and guarantees of our God, that He is who He is said to be, and His deliverables are as exact as His attributes are! Hence Jeremiah's prayer.

Jeremiah's prayer listed above simply highlights God's attributes-declaring God's power and testimonies of His previous works. God in response to Jeremiah's declarations, acknowledges and asserts His attributes, by saying in Jeremiah 32:27: "**Behold, I am the Lord, the God of all flesh; is there anything too hard for Me?**" (see Jeremiah 32:27; NKJV). God then proceeds with outlining how He will restore Israel based on His ability as the God of all possibilities, through the covenant He has with Israel.

Jeremiah's prayer is not only a great example, but a testimony of God standing by His Word, and responding to our prayers. We also know that we serve an unchanging God. According to Numbers 23:19, *"God is not man, that he should lie, or a son of man, that he should change his mind. Has he said, and will he not do it? Or has he spoken, and will he not fulfill it"* ([8]ESV). If God can respond to prayers that acknowledged His power and abilities with Jeremiah, He will respond to our prayers as well. This is the power of praying the attributes of God!

---

[8] Scripture quotations identified throughout this book in KJV (King James Version), NKJV (New King James Versions), NLT (New Living Translation Version), AMPC(Amplified Version Classic Edition), ESV(English Standard Version), NIV(New International Version), and NASB (New American Standard Bible) and others indicated are from www.biblegateway.com

GOD MY FATHER

CHAPTER 2

Luke 11:2- So He said to them, "When you pray, say: Our Father in heaven, Hallowed be Your name. Your kingdom come; Your will be done on earth as it is in heaven (NKJV).

Scripture Application

As believers we pray directly to God. Jesus Christ reconciled us to direct communication and relationship with God our Creator and Father. Jesus, in Luke 11:2, instructed us to pray to God the Father. While He was on earth Jesus frequently secluded himself to pray. Scripture also tells us that Jesus only did what He saw His Father doing. *"So Jesus said to them, "truly, truly, I say to you, the Son can do nothing of his own accord, but only what he sees the Father doing. For whatever the Father does, that the Son does likewise. For the Father loves the Son and shows him all that he himself is doing. And greater works than these will he show him, so that you may marvel"* (John 5:19-20, ESV).

When we accepted Jesus Christ as Lord and Savior, we became sons and daughters of God. We can now relate to God as our creator and Father. There is uniqueness to God as Father, he is ever loving, he does not rebuke us to condemn us, but instead chastens us to make us better. God does not recall our sins; he forgets them as soon as we repent. God does not deal with us according to our level of righteousness or sins, he is fair in his dealings with us. God shows no partiality, he loves all mankind equally. Psalm 103 is a great reminder of God's goodness as a Father. Let me just highlight some verses here that express these attributes: *"Bless the Lord, O my soul, and forget not all his benefits, who forgives all your iniquity, who heals all your diseases, who redeems your life from the pit, who crowns you with steadfast love and mercy, who satisfies you with good so that your youth is renewed like the eagle's. The Lord is merciful and gracious, slow to anger and abounding in steadfast love. He will not always chide, nor will he keep his anger forever. He does not deal with us according to our sins, nor repay us according to our iniquities. For as high as the heavens are above the earth, so great is his steadfast love toward those who fear him; as far as the east is from the west, so far does he remove our transgressions from us. As a father shows compassion to his children, so the Lord shows compassion to those who fear him"* (Psalm 103:1-5; 8-14; ESV).

Depending on our upbringing in church, family, or culture, at times, we may relate to God the way we relate to our earthly fathers or persons of authority. However, God is different, we can relate to him knowing that His mercies and compassion towards us will never cease. If you grew up without a father, know that God is a Father to the fatherless. If you were abandoned, know that you are accepted of the Lord. God has no illegitimate or unwanted children. He is our creator and we are all His children. Confidently we can call Him Abba Father.

As the good Father, God has the best in mind for us. *"You parents—if your children ask for a loaf of bread, do you give them a stone instead? Or if they ask for a fish, do you give them a snake? Of course not! So, if you sinful people know how to give good gifts to your children, how much more will your heavenly Father give good gifts to those who ask him"* (Matthew 7:9-11; NLT). As a Father, God also directs each of us in the ways we should go. His eyes are always on us (see Psalm 32:8, NKJV).

Despite the population of the world God loves each of us individually. Unlike a large family, where some children may be favored more than others, the Father knows each one of us individually. He knows each hair strand on our heads! Each person has an individualized plan that was developed by our Father for successful completion of each of our destinies. As the good Father that He is, God predestined us, planning for us in advance, even before we were born. These are peaceful plans. Plans that give us hope and a future (see Jeremiah 29:11, NKJV).

We can, therefore, come to God in prayer and in fellowship, confidently knowing that He is a Father who looks forward to hearing from us. In Jeremiah 29:13, God says, *"You will seek Me and find Me when you search for Me with all your heart"* (NASB). Jesus in Matthew 7:7, says *"Ask, and it will be given to you; seek, and you will find; knock, and it will be opened to you"* (NASB). He is a Father who wants to connect with each of us, even at our lowest points. The high and lofty one who lives in eternity, the Holy One, says this, *"I live in the high and holy place with those whose spirits are contrite and humble. I restore the crushed spirit of the humble and revive the courage of those with repentant hearts"* (Isaiah 57:15; NLT).

As you read this book and pray along; be assured that God, as Father, will not ignore you. You are a son or daughter of God who catches His attention whenever you call on him in fellowship. 1 John 5:14-15: *"And we are confident that he hears us whenever we ask for anything that pleases him. And since we know he hears us when we make our requests, we also know that he will give us what we ask for"* (ESV).

Scriptures of Affirmation
The Almighty God is my Father

- Romans 8: 15-17: For you did not receive the spirit of bondage again to fear, but you received the Spirit of adoption by whom we cry out, "Abba, Father." The Spirit Himself bears witness with our spirit that we are children of God and if children, then heirs—heirs of God and joint heirs with Christ, if indeed we suffer with Him, that we may also be glorified together (NKJV).

- Matthew 6:6: But you, when you pray, go into your room, and when you have shut your door, pray to your Father who is in the secret place; and your Father who sees in secret will reward you openly (NKJV).

- Isaiah 63: 16: For you are our Father, though Abraham does not know us, and Israel does not acknowledge us; you, O LORD, are our Father, our Redeemer from of old is your name (ESV).

- Psalm 64:4-5: Sing to God, sing praises to His name; Extol Him who rides on the clouds, By His name Yah and rejoice before Him. A father of the fatherless, a defender of widows, Is God in His holy habitation (NKJV).

- Psalm 27:10: Even if my father and mother abandon me, the Lord will hold me close (NLT).

- Galatians 4:3-7: Even so we, when we were children, were in bondage under the elements of the world. But when the fullness of the time had come, God sent forth His Son, born of a woman, born under the law, to redeem those who were under the law, that **we might receive the adoption as sons**. and because you are sons, God has sent forth the Spirit of His Son into your hearts, crying **out, "Abba, Father**! "Therefore, you are no longer a slave but a son, and if a son, then an heir of God through Christ (NKJV).

- Jeremiah 31:33: But this is the new covenant I will make with the people of Israel after those days," says the Lord. "I will put my instructions deep within them, and I will write them on their hearts. **I will be their God, and they will be my people**. And they will not need to teach their neighbors, nor will they need to teach their relatives, saying, 'You should know the Lord.' **For everyone, from the least to the greatest, will know me already," says the Lord. "And I will forgive their wickedness, and I will never again remember their sins** (NLT).

- Psalm 139:13-18: For You formed my inward parts; You covered me in my mother's womb. I will praise You, for I am fearfully and wonderfully made; Marvelous are Your works, and that my soul knows very well. My frame was not hidden from You, when I was made in secret, and skillfully wrought in the lowest parts of the earth. Your eyes saw my substance, being yet unformed and in Your book they all were written, the days fashioned for me, when as yet there were none of them. How precious also are Your thoughts to me, O God! How great is the sum of them! If I should count them, they would be more in number than the sand; When I awake, I am still with You (⁹NKJV).

Prayer

Father God, I embrace you as my Father. I thank you, for reconciling and adopting me as your son or daughter through Jesus Christ. I thank you, for my new identity in you. I honor you, and I am grateful that I have free access to you; and that I can reach you at any time. I thank you, for the plans that you have for me, and the guidance of your right hand and of your eyes over my life. I am grateful that you only have the best in mind for me. I celebrate the freedom and the joy that I find in you, because you are not a threatening Father but a welcoming One. I accept you as my Father and agree with everything you have planned for my life. I thank You Lord for peace, hope, and for the success of my life. In Jesus Name, Amen.

---

⁹ Scripture quotations identified throughout this book in KJV (King James Version), NKJV (New King James Versions), NLT (New Living Translation Version), AMPC(Amplified Version Classic Edition), ESV(English Standard Version), NIV(New International Version), and NASB (New American Standard Bible) and others indicated are from www.biblegateway.com

GOD WHO LOVES ME

Jeremiah 31:3- The Lord has appeared of old to me, saying: Yes, I have loved you with an everlasting love; therefore, with lovingkindness I have drawn you (NKJV).

Scripture Application

I struggled for a long time with accepting God's love. Although I was born again, I thought God was harsh and punitive. In times of hardship and adversity I often viewed what was happening to me as punishment from God. I was constantly under condemnation, shame, and quilt. The words "I love you" were not spoken in my family until late in my adulthood. Growing up in a single-family home, life was more about survival and ensuring that basic needs were met. It was not until late 2009, when God started preparing me for ministry, that I embraced God's love. God had to break those wrong beliefs off me, privately, in my early thirties during a season of prayer.

Since then I have continued to walk in the fullness of the wonderful promises of God's Love. I have come to learn and accept that God is not mad at me; if I sin, I can quickly reconcile with Him through repentance. To know that God does not deal with me because of my sins was a huge deliverance. Major chains of bondages were broken in 2009. That is why I love Psalm 103, the entire chapter; it was one of the key Scriptures that convinced me of God's love.

God's love is unconditional. He accepts us as we are. We do not have to prove anything or work out anything to get noticed and accepted by God, because He sees everything, knows everything, and sees everyone. There is such peace and joy when you are loved by God. There is freedom of communication and interaction; you can share secrets and exchange ideas freely. There are no fears of betrayals or disappointments; you are enriched and edified by such a relationship. No wonder we can call him the Friend who sticks closer than a brother (see Proverbs 18:24; NKJV).

You see in God's love we have the confidence that nothing can separate us from this love (see Romans 8:31-39)! So, in prayer, we can come to Him boldly, knowing that our God is approachable-He will never shun us - we have the liberty to draw near to Him in time of need. Hebrews 4:16 says *"Therefore let us draw near with confidence to the throne of grace, so that we may receive mercy and find grace to help in time of need"* (NASB). *"Praise the Lord. Give thanks to the Lord, for He is good; His love endures forever"* (Psalm 106:1; NASB).

Scriptures of Affirmation
I am Loved by God

- John 3:16: For God so loved the world that He gave His only begotten Son, that whoever believes in Him should not perish but have everlasting life (NKJV).

- Deuteronomy 7:9: Know therefore that the Lord your God is God; he is the faithful God, keeping his covenant of love to a thousand generations of those who love him and keep his commandments (NIV).

- Romans 8:31:33: What then shall we say to these things? If God is for us, who can be against us? He who did not spare His own Son, but delivered Him up for us all, how shall He not with Him also freely give us all things? 33 Who shall bring a charge against God's elect? It is God who justifies (NKJV).

- Ephesians 2:4-5: But because of his great love for us, God, who is rich in mercy, 5 made us alive with Christ even when we were dead in transgressions—it is by grace you have been saved (NIV).

- Romans 8:38-39: For I am persuaded that neither death nor life, nor angels nor principalities nor powers, nor things present nor things to come, 39 nor height nor depth, nor any other created thing, shall be able to separate us from the love of God which is in Christ Jesus our Lord (NJKV).

- 1 John 3:1: See what kind of love the Father has given to us, that we should be called children of God; and so, we are. The reason why the world does not know us is that it did not know him (ESV).

- Daniel 9:4: I prayed to the Lord my God and confessed: Lord, the great and awesome God, who keeps his covenant of love with those who love him and keep his commandments (NIV).

- Song of Solomon 6:3: I AM my beloved's and my beloved is Mine He who pastures his flock among the lilies. ([10]NASB).

---

[10] Scripture quotations identified throughout this book in KJV (King James Version), NKJV (New King James Versions), NLT (New Living Translation Version), AMPC(Amplified Version Classic Edition), ESV(English Standard Version), NIV(New International Version), and NASB (New American Standard Bible) and others indicated are from www.biblegateway.com

Prayer

Father God, I thank you for being a good Father who loves me unconditionally. I embrace your love. I thank you, for loving me just the way I am and for creating me this way. I repent of any areas I have doubted your love for me. I repent of any situation, action, or word that I have expressed unlovingly towards others. I renounce hatred, envy, prejudice of any kind and self-hatred. I ask for your forgiveness. Now Lord I embrace your love, I forgive anyone who has said or acted unlovingly towards me. I forgive them for hurting me and I let them go. Father show me how to love myself and how to love others. Show me how to minister to others in love. Let your love be my measuring stick to apply to every situation. Lord, show me how to love in challenging situations. Show me how to love difficult people. Teach me how to love my enemies. Lord, continue to teach me your ways that I may impact many with your love. I bless and thank you, for your endless love and I accept your love. In Jesus Name, Amen

THE HOLY GOD

CHAPTER 4

*Leviticus 19: 2-*The Lord said to Moses, Speak to the entire assembly of Israel and say to them: Be holy because I, the Lord your God, am holy (NIV).

Scripture Application

For a born-again believer, I believe holiness is an attitude or posture of the mind and heart, and a lifestyle. Holiness transcends beyond external presentation. It influences our character, speech, and actions. Holiness also influences our attitude towards God in service to others, as well as communicating with Him.

Our attitude in prayer and in relationship with God should be one of reverence and honor. Remember prayer is talking to God; prayer is fellowship. It is not a monologue it is a dialogue, between two entities. This requires that we position ourselves well to engage in this fellowship with God. Part of the attitude of reverence includes the aligning of all of our faculties to engage with God during prayer. Set your mind, emotions, body, heart, spirit, and senses to engage with God and the Holy Spirit during prayer. It is important to do this to combat distractions that can occur while you are praying

It is best to start prayer in worship and reverence. Take ample time worshiping and praising God. Invite the Holy Spirit, angels, and the heavenly host in worship as well. Repentance is a key factor as we approach God's holiness in prayer. So, factor repentance into your prayer by repenting of sins, transgressions or iniquities, and anything else the Holy Spirit brings to your attention. This is where you can also ask the Holy Spirit to search your heart for anything that needs repentance. But repentance should not be set aside for prayer time only; make it a habit to repent whenever you are convicted by the Holy Spirit.

Finally, purpose to stay engaged with the Holy Spirit. Prayer opens the atmosphere for God's presence. God talks and moves profoundly when we are in His presence. Also, note that the heavenly host, angels, and Jesus Christ are also present during prayer, so stay alert, talk to God in prayer, but also wait for Him to talk to you. Continue to reverence and honor God wherever you are.

Scriptures of Affirmation
Only God is Holy and worthy of my Worship

- Exodus 15:11: Who is like you, O Lord, among the gods? Who is like you, majestic in holiness, awesome in glorious deeds, doing wonders? (ESV).

- Psalm 96.9: Worship the Lord in the splendor of holiness; tremble before him, all the earth! (ESV).

- Isaiah 35:8: And a highway shall be there, and it shall be called the Way of Holiness; the unclean shall not pass over it. It shall belong to those who walk on the way; even if they are fools, they shall not go astray (ESV).

- 1 Samuel 2: 2: There is none holy like the Lord; there is none besides you; there is no rock like our God (ESV).

- Isaiah 6:1-4: In the year that King Uzziah died, I saw the Lord, high and exalted, seated on a throne; and the train of his robe filled the temple. Above him were seraphim, each with six wings: With two wings they covered their faces, with two they covered their feet, and with two they were flying. And they were calling to one another: Holy, holy, holy is the Lord Almighty; the whole earth is full of his glory. At the sound of their voices the doorposts and thresholds shook, and the temple was filled with smoke (NIV).

- 1 John 3:3: And everyone who thus hopes in him purifies himself as he is pure (ESV).

- 2 Corinthian 2: 1: Since we have these promises, beloved, let us cleanse ourselves from every defilement of body and spirit, bringing holiness to completion in the fear of God (ESV).

- 1 Peter 1: 15-16: But as he who called you is holy, you also be holy in all your conduct, since it is written, You shall be holy, for I am holy (ESV).

- Romans 12:1: I appeal to you therefore, brothers, by the mercies of God, to present your bodies as a living sacrifice, holy and acceptable to God, which is your spiritual worship (ESV).1 Peter 2:9: But you are a chosen race, a royal priesthood, a holy nation, a people for his own possession, that you may proclaim the excellencies of him who called you out of darkness into his marvelous light (ESV).

- 1 Peter 1:13-16: Therefore, preparing your minds for action, and being sober-minded, set your hope fully on the grace that will be brought to you at the revelation of Jesus Christ. As obedient children, do not be conformed to the passions of your former ignorance, but as he who called you is holy, you also be holy in all your conduct, since it is written, You shall be holy, for I am holy (ESV).

- 1 John 1:5: This is the message we have heard from him and proclaim to you, that God is light, and in him is no darkness at all (ESV).

- Revelation 4: 6-11: Before the throne there was a sea of glass, like crystal. And in the midst of the throne, and around the throne, were four living creatures full of eyes in front and in back. The first living creature was like a lion, the second living creature like a calf, the third living creature had a face like a man, and the fourth living creature was like a flying eagle. The four living creatures, each having six wings, were full of eyes around and within. And they do not rest day or night, saying: Holy, holy, holy, Lord God Almighty, Who was and is and is to come! Whenever the living creatures give glory and honor and thanks to Him who sits on the throne, who lives forever and ever, the twenty-four elders fall down before Him who sits on the throne and worship Him who lives forever and ever, and cast their crowns before the throne, saying: You are worthy, O Lord, to receive glory and honor and power. For You created all things, and by Your will they exist and were created ([11]NKJV).

Prayer

Father, in Jesus Name, I worship and adore you. I declare that you are the Almighty God, the One God, worthy of worship and adoration. I worship you. I join with the heavenly hosts and the twenty-four elders in worship, declaring that you are holy, holy, holy, there is none like you Lord. Thank you, God, that you are willing to reside in the praises of your people. Thank you, God, that you want to reside in me and thank you for making

---

[11] Scripture quotations identified throughout this book in KJV (King James Version), NKJV (New King James Versions), NLT (New Living Translation Version), AMPC(Amplified Version Classic Edition), ESV(English Standard Version), NIV(New International Version), and NASB (New American Standard Bible) and others indicated are from www.biblegateway.com

me a holy vessel before you. Lord, I now commit to be holy; I commit everything in my life as holy unto you. I commit my home, my vehicle, my marriage, my finances, my children, my business, my job, and my office holy unto you. I commit my appearance and presentation, my speech, and actions, holy unto you. I worship you with everything I have. I worship you in the beauty of your holiness. You are holy God; I worship and adore you. In Jesus Name. Amen

GOD THE I AM
I AM WHO I AM

Exodus 3:14-15- Then Moses said to God, Indeed, when I come to the children of Israel and say to them, The God of your fathers has sent me to you, and they say to me, What is His name? what shall I say to them? And God said to Moses, I AM WHO I AM. And He said, Thus you shall say to the children of Israel, **I AM** has sent me to you (NKJV).

Scripture Application

When I look at God as the I AM, I just get overwhelmed by His awesomeness. Words are not enough to describe what that Name really means, other than, He is what He says He is. I consider I AM the all-inclusiveness of God, His ability, His might, His power, His love, but even more so, the Ever-Present Solution in time of need. In the Old Testament, God often described Himself as the solution the Israelites needed as they journeyed to the promise land, and that still applies to us today. God describes Himself as I AM on many occasions, for example, in deliverance, salvation and redemption, (see Exodus 6:7) *"I will take you as my own people, and I will be your God. Then you will know* ***that I am the Lord your God,*** *who brought you out from under the yoke of* the Egyptians" (NIV). Leviticus 20:24: *"I am the Lord your God, who has set you apart from the nation"* (NIV).

God, the I AM, is ever present and unchanging. He is available and ready to meet us at our point of need. This makes fellowship and prayer much easier because we know we have an ever-available God. God will never put us on hold when we call on Him. Deuteronomy 4:7 says, *"For what great nation is there that has a god so **near to it as the LORD our God** is to us, whenever we call upon Him?"* (ESV). God is already near to hear and to respond to that which we need. So, when we approach Him in fellowship or in prayer, we have this assurance, that I AM – the one Who has the best solution is already there to provide. I AM, the all sufficient God of provision. If God is all sufficient, what more can we offer Him, other than, praise, worship, and thanksgiving:

Scriptures of Affirmation
My God is Matchless

- Psalm 29:1-2: Ascribe to the Lord, O heavenly beings, ascribe to the Lord glory and strength. Ascribe to the Lord the glory due his name; worship the Lord in the splendor of holiness (ESV).

- Jude 1: 25: To God our Savior, who alone is wise be glory and majesty, dominion, and power both now and forever. Amen (NKJV).

- Isaiah 43:13: Even from eternity I am He, and there is none who can deliver out of My hand; I act and who can reverse it (NASB).

- John 8:58: Jesus said unto them, Verily, verily, I say unto you, Before Abraham was, I am (KJV).

- Isaiah 9:6: His Name will be called Wonderful, Counselor, Mighty God, Everlasting Father, Prince of Peace (NKJV).

- Nehemiah 9:6: You alone are the LORD You have made the heavens, The heaven of heavens with all their host, the earth and all that is on it, the seas and all that is in them You give life to all of them And the heavenly host bows down before You (NASB).

- Revelation 4:11: You are worthy, our Lord and God, to receive glory and honor and power, for you created all things, and by your will they were created and have their being (NIV).

- Revelation 4:8: The four living creatures, each having six wings, were full of eyes around and within. And they do not rest day or night, saying: Holy, holy, holy, Lord God Almighty, who was and is and is to come (NKJV).

- Revelation 5:13-14: And every creature which is in heaven and on the earth and under the earth and such as are in the sea, and all that are in them, I heard saying: "Blessing and honor and glory and power Be to Him who sits on the throne, and to the Lamb, forever and ever Then the four living creatures said, "Amen!" And the twenty-four elders fell down and worshiped Him who lives forever and ever ([12]NKJV).

Prayer

Lord God, I worship you, and honor, and adore you. I worship you, All Sufficient God, who knows everything about me, and has everything ready for me. I worship and exalt you for providing every need of my life, as I walk in obedience to you. I thank you, God, for supplying my physical, financial, emotional, and psychological needs. Thank you,

---

[12] Scripture quotations identified throughout this book in KJV (King James Version), NKJV (New King James Versions), NLT (New Living Translation Version), AMPC(Amplified Version Classic Edition), ESV(English Standard Version), NIV(New International Version), and NASB (New American Standard Bible) and others indicated are from www.biblegateway.com

Lord, for protection, provision, guidance, deliverance, healing, salvation, restitution, and restoration. Thank you, for companionship, comfort, and friendship. I worship and adore you. I honor you. You are excellent, majestic, glorious. Thank you, for your counsel and wisdom, revelation, and insight, understanding and might. Thank you, for life and wellbeing. Thank you, for satisfying my desires. Thank you, for responding to my needs with exceedingly more than I might ask or think. I bless you Lord, I adore you, I worship you. You are holy, you are wonderful, you are great. Holy, holy, holy is the Lord God Almighty, The Lord, the I AM, my heavenly Father.

THE ALMIGHTY GOD
ALL POWERFUL GOD
JEHOVAH EL SHADDAI
OMNIPOTENT GOD

CHAPTER 6

Genesis 17:1- When Abram was ninety-nine years old the Lord appeared to Abram and said to him, I am God Almighty; walk before me, and be blameless (ESV).

Scripture Application

This name is one of the names, that has impacted my life profoundly. There was a period of time when I was in a season of great adversity. One morning after prayer, as I was leaving my prayer room, I had a strong conviction; I heard my spirit boldly and powerfully say, "the Almighty God is My Father." I had absolute assurance from that moment on that all things were possible with God, and that nothing was too overwhelming for Him to handle. The other aspect of this Name was the fact, He is my Father. The Creator of the universe, who holds everything in place, and sets boundaries, the incomparable God, is my Father. I grew up fatherless, and to know that I had the Almighty God to run to, to embrace, to seek counsel from, and protection from, made a huge difference for me. I typed the words, in large and bold letters, "The Almighty God is My Father" with the date of the occurrence and posted them in my office where they remained up to the day, I left the workforce.

God as El Shaddai means Mighty Provider who nourishes, supplies, and satisfies every need of His children even needs that were otherwise deemed impossible to have been met. El Shaddai is capable of providing every need. Other names that speak of God's magnificence are, Elohim which means God creator and judge and El Gibbor which stands for Mighty God, the only all-powerful God.

These words were constant reminders of Who was for me, and of His mighty power to lead, protect, shelter, and provide for me. God, the I AM, the Almighty God- El Shaddai covers all areas of our lives. Omni means all, potent means all powerful. He is The Self-Sufficient God, with unlimited resources. He does exceptionally above what we ask or expect. Trust God's unparalleled power and ability for your situation as well.

Scriptures of Affirmation
My God is powerful

- Isaiah 44: 24-26a: Thus says the Lord, your Redeemer and He who formed you from the womb: **I am the Lord, who makes all things,** Who stretches out the heavens all alone, Who spreads abroad the earth by Myself; Who frustrates the signs of the babblers, and drives diviners mad; Who turns wise men backward, and makes their knowledge foolishness; **Who confirms the word of His servant and performs the counsel of His messengers** (NKJV).

- Revelation 19:6: Then I heard what seemed to be the voice of a great multitude, like the roar of many waters and like the sound of mighty peals of thunder, crying out, Hallelujah! For the Lord, our God the Almighty reigns (ESV).

- Genesis 14:19: And he blessed him and said, blessed be Abram by God Most High, Possessor of heaven and earth (ESV).

- Deuteronomy 10:17: For the Lord, your God is **God of gods and Lord of lords, the great, the mighty, and the awesome God,** who is not partial and takes no bribe (ESV).

- 1 Chronicles 29:11: Yours, O LORD, is the greatness and the power and the glory and the victory and the majesty, indeed everything that is in the heavens and the earth; Yours is the dominion, O LORD, and You exalt Yourself as head over all (NASB).

- Matthew 19:26: But Jesus looked at them and said, With man this is impossible, but with God all things are possible (ESV).

- Luke 1:37: For nothing will be impossible with God (ESV).

- Philippians 4:13: I can do all things through Christ who strengthens me (NKJV).

- 2 Chronicles 20:6: And he said, O LORD, the God of our fathers, are You not God in the heavens? And are You not ruler over all the kingdoms of the nations? Power and might are in Your hand so that no one can stand against You (NASB).

- Job 9:4-9: **God is wise in heart and mighty in strength.** Who has hardened himself against Him and prospered? He removes the mountains, and they do not know When He overturns them in His anger; He shakes the earth out of its place, and its pillars tremble; He commands the sun, and it does not rise; He seals off the stars; He alone spreads out the heavens, And treads on the waves of the sea; He made the Bear, Orion, and the Pleiades, and the chambers of the south; He does great things past finding out, Yes, wonders without number (NKJV).

- Jeremiah 32:17: Ah, Lord God! It is you who have made the heavens and the earth by your great power and by your outstretched arm! Nothing is too hard for you (ESV).

- Genesis 18:14: Is anything too hard for the Lord? At the appointed time I will return to you, about this time next year, and Sarah shall have a son (ESV).

- Ephesians 3:20-21: Now to Him who is able to do exceedingly abundantly above all that we ask or think, according to the power that works in us, 21 to Him be glory in the church by Christ Jesus to all generations, forever and ever. Amen (NKJV).

- Isaiah 40:28: Have you not known? Have you not heard? The everlasting God, the Lord, the Creator of the ends of the earth, neither faints nor is weary. His understanding is unsearchable (NKJV).

- Revelation 19:11-16: After that I saw heaven opened, and behold, a white horse appeared! The One Who was riding it is called Faithful (Trustworthy, Loyal, Incorruptible, Steady) and True, and He passes judgment and wages war in righteousness (holiness, justice, and uprightness). His eyes [blaze] like a flame of fire, and on His head are many kingly crowns (diadems); and He has a title (name) inscribed which He alone knows or can understand. He is dressed in a robe dyed by dipping in blood, and the title by which He is called is The Word of God and the troops of heaven, clothed in fine linen, dazzling and clean, followed Him on white horses. From His mouth goes forth a sharp sword with which He can smite (afflict, strike) the nations; and He will shepherd and control them with a staff (scepter, rod) of iron. He will tread the winepress of the fierceness of the wrath and indignation of God the All-Ruler -the Almighty, the Omnipotent (AMPC).

Prayer

Almighty God, I acknowledge you as my Father. I acknowledge you as the All-Powerful God, creator of earth and heaven and everything in it. You are mighty in strength and power; all things are possible with you. There is nothing too difficult for you. There is no situation in my life that you cannot handle. I repent Lord, for trusting my will and ability to fix problems. Forgive me God, for my independence and self-reliance. I now submit to you God as the Almighty, all-powerful God. I submit my needs to you; acknowledging your ability to resolve and bring answers to these situations. I thank you Lord, that when I seek you, I find you, when I ask, you answer, when I knock, you open. Thank you, Lord, for bringing answers to my needs, exceedingly, abundantly above all that I have petitioned for. I receive with thanksgiving, in Jesus Name, Amen.[13]

[13] Scripture quotations identified throughout this book in KJV (King James Version), NKJV (New King James Versions), NLT (New Living Translation Version), AMPC(Amplified Version Classic Edition), ESV(English Standard Version), NIV(New International Version), and NASB (New American Standard Bible) and others indicated are from www.biblegateway.com

THE LORD - YAHWEH JEHOVAH ADONAI

Exodus 6:2-3-God spoke to Moses and said to him, "I am the Lord. I appeared to Abraham, to Isaac, and to Jacob, as God Almighty, but by **My name the Lord** I did not make myself known to them (ESV).

Scripture Application

The context of Exodus 6:1-9 is about God renewing His covenant with the Israelites, and His promise to deliver them from captivity. *"And God spoke to Moses and said to him: "I am the Lord. I appeared to Abraham, to Isaac, and to Jacob, as God Almighty, **but by My name Lord I was not known to them**. I have also established My covenant with them, to give them the land of Canaan, the land of their pilgrimage, in which they were strangers. And I have also heard the groaning of the children of Israel whom the Egyptians keep in bondage, and I have remembered My covenant. Therefore, say to the children of Israel: '**I am the Lord;** <u>I will bring you out from under the burdens of the Egyptians, I will rescue you from their bondage, and I will redeem you with an outstretched arm and with great judgments</u>. I will take you as My people, and I will be your God. **Then you shall know that I am the Lord your God who brings you out from under the burdens of the Egyptians**. And I will bring you into the land which I swore to give to Abraham, Isaac, and*

Jacob; and I will give it to you as a heritage: I am the Lord. So, Moses spoke thus to the children of Israel; but they did not heed Moses, because of anguish of spirit and cruel bondage" (NKJV).

Where Scripture says "but by My Name the Lord I was not known to them" implies to me, another side or attribute of God that the Israelites did not know, and were about to experience, through this deliverance and restorative process. **Adonai in Hebrew means my Lord OR my Master, Owner, OR Sovereign ruler.** Adonai can be applied interchangeably with **Jehovah El Elyon;** which means Most High; Possessor of heaven and earth. This implies authority as well as the high and exalted place God inhabits. Before and throughout their exodus the Israelites witnessed God's power through plagues that affected the Egyptians; through His divine protection and guidance in the wilderness; through His mighty power in war fighting their enemies; through miraculous provision of food and water; through preservation of their clothing; and also through God's judgement for disobedience, rebellion and grumbling. The Israelites experienced the Lordship of God, as a good Father, through love and discipline. God maintained His Lordship until they entered the promised land. To date we still have His Lordship, guiding, protecting, preserving, providing, and delivering us.

God has not changed. Our covenant with Him was reinstated through the atonement of the Blood of Jesus Christ. As born-again believers we now have a new covenant. Philippians 1:6, says "That He who began a good work in you, will bring it to completion (NIV)." We still have a destiny to complete, promises to grab and live out to fullness; and our God will see us through when we submit to His Lordship. We have no other Lord but God, no other provider but God, no other deliverer but God. For whatever issue we may have, let us submit it to God's Lordship.

Scriptures of Affirmation:
Yahweh is my God and My Lord

- Psalm 83:18: That they may know that you alone, whose name is the Lord, are the Most High over all the earth (ESV).

- Isaiah 42:8: I am the Lord; that is my name; my glory I give to no other, nor my praise to carved idols. (ESV).

- Jeremiah 32:27: Behold, I am the LORD, the God of all flesh; is anything too difficult for Me?" (ESV).

- Psalm 114:7-8: Tremble, O earth, at the presence of the Lord, at the presence of the God of Jacob, who turns the rock into a pool of water, the flint into a spring of water (ESV). Also read the entire chapter of Psalm 114.

- Isaiah 1:24: Therefore, says the Lord, the Lord of hosts, the Mighty One of Israel, Ah, I will appease Myself on My adversaries and avenge Myself on My enemies (AMPC).

- Revelation 19:16: And on His garment (robe) and on His thigh He has a name (title) inscribed, King of kings and Lord of lords (AMPC).

- Philippians 2: 9-11: Therefore God also has highly exalted Him and given Him the name which is above every name, that at the name of Jesus every knee should bow, of those in heaven, and of those on earth, and of those under the earth, and that every tongue should confess that Jesus Christ is Lord, to the glory of God the Father ([14]NKJV).

---

[14] Scripture quotations identified throughout this book in KJV (King James Version), NKJV (New King James Versions), NLT (New Living Translation Version), AMPC(Amplified Version Classic Edition), ESV(English Standard Version), NIV(New International Version), and NASB (New American Standard Bible) and others indicated are from www.biblegateway.com

Prayer

Adonai God, I acknowledge you as LORD. I acknowledge you as my Lord. Father God, I thank you, for the mighty works you have done in the past. I thank you, for wars you have fought on my behalf to deliver and protect me. I bless you, for the mighty works you have in store for me for the future. I trust you as my deliverer and as my Lord. I acknowledge your strong Right Hand that rests upon me to save and protect me from harm. I pray now that the Cloud of your presence will go before me. I pray that your glory will be my rear guard. I pray that Your fire will go before me. Lord, arise and let my enemies be scattered. Thank you, Jesus, for overcoming all on my behalf. I turn every battle over to you and ask that your Spirit raise up a standard against my adversaries. Lord, part the waters that need be, make ways in the deserts where need be, engage your creation to work on my behalf. Let your power be manifested in my life for your glory. In Jesus Name, I pray, Amen!

THE OMNISCIENT
THE ALL-KNOWING GOD

Romans 11:33-36- Oh, the depth of the riches both of the wisdom and knowledge of God! How unsearchable are His judgments and His ways past finding out! For who has known the mind of the Lord? Or who has become His counselor? "Or who has first given to Him and it shall be repaid to him?" For of Him and through Him and to Him are all things, to whom be glory forever. Amen (NJKV).

Scripture Application

Human nature desires to know things in advance. Technology has made information readily available through just a push of buttons on smart phones, laptops, or tablets. Despite advances in science, technology, and human knowledge we are still limited to how much we know. There are still medical conditions that are incurable unless God intervenes. In life we may face unexplainable situations that only God knows and sees.

I have relied on the All-Knowing God when I cannot understand some situations or when I have exhausted searching for solutions to problems. I should just take such issues to God first before embarking on the search! I have also called on the All-Seeing God whenever I have been misunderstood or accused wrongly. The All-Seeing God sees everything and everyone. There is nothing hidden from His sight. Hebrews 4:13 says *"That nothing in all creation is hidden from God's sight. Everything is uncovered and laid bare before the eyes of him to whom we must give account"* (NIV).

I have also depended on the All-Knowing, All Seeing God for matters of the heart and for things that are hidden that need exposure; Jeremiah 17:10 says "I, the Lord, search the heart, I test the mind, even to give every man according to his ways, according to the fruit of his doings" (ESV). 1Chronicles 28:9 is a great Scripture for evaluating personal motives and for exposing wrong motives of others. It says ***"As for you, my son Solomon, know the God of your father, and serve Him with a whole heart and a willing mind; for the LORD searches all hearts, and understands every intent of the thoughts. If you seek Him, He will let you find Him; but if you forsake Him, He will reject you forever"*** (NASB).

Have you ever lost something and asked the Lord to locate it for you? When you have run out of all options, or when you need to understand something, trust the Omniscient God. When you are looking for something, or when you have been misunderstood, trust the All-Seeing God. Let me end this section with a testimony. A lady in a discipleship group shared that she lived in an apartment complex whose foundation needed to be excavated due to leakage from a pipe. The leak was caused by a blockage, and they could see what blocked the pipe, but could not remove it. The excavation was going to be so costly and likely bankrupt the apartment complex. So, the night before the excavation the lady prayed saying *"Lord, you see where the blockage is, You are the Lord who sees. Remove that blockage and save the complex from going bankrupt, in Jesus Name."* Well the next morning, the president of the apartment complex went to check the pipe and noticed that the blockage was not there! There was no need to excavate the foundation to replace the sewage pipe. Glory to God! Glory to the Lord who sees!

Scriptures of Affirmation
My God is has knowledge of everything

- Psalm 139:4: Even before there is a word on my tongue, behold, O Lord, You know it all (NASB).

- 1 John 3:20: For if our heart condemns us, God is greater than our heart, and knows all things (NKJV).

- Psalm 147:4-5: He counts the number of the stars; He gives names to all of them. Great is our Lord and abundant in strength; His understanding is infinite (NASB).

- Psalm 44:20-21: If we had forgotten the name of our God or extended our hands to a strange god, would not God find this out? For He knows the secrets of the heart (NASB).

- Psalm 139:1-6: O Lord, You have searched me and known me. You know when I sit down and when I rise up; You understand my thought from afar. You scrutinize my path and my lying down and are intimately acquainted with all my ways. Even before there is a word on my tongue, Behold, O Lord, You know it all. You have enclosed me behind and before and laid Your hand upon me. Such knowledge is too wonderful for me; It is too high; I cannot attain to it (NASB).

- Psalm 139:15-18a: My frame was not hidden from You, when I was made in secret and skillfully wrought in the depths of the earth; Your eyes have seen my unformed substance and in Your book were all written. The days that were ordained for me, when as yet there was not one of them. How precious also are Your thoughts to me, O God! How vast is the sum of them! If I should count them, they would outnumber the sand (NASB).

- 1 Corinthians 2:11: For who knows a person's thoughts except their own spirit within them? In the same way no one knows the thoughts of God except the Spirit of God ([15]NIV).

Prayer

Father, in the Name of Jesus, I thank and worship you, as the All-Knowing, All-seeing God. I thank you, for the answers to things I do not know or understand. Thank you, Lord, that in your time you will give me the information I need, and the wisdom to do what you me to do. I am content with what I know, and with what I do not know. I, also, thank you, that you see all things, nothing is hidden from your sight, vindicate me and avenge me against misunderstandings or false accusations. Father, since you see everything, show me, what I need to know. Open my eyes to see what you want me to see. Lord, search my heart, and my thoughts, and remove anything that is standing in your way. Create in me a new heart, oh Lord, remove a heart of stone, replace it with a heart of flesh. Let the Blood of Jesus cleanse my thoughts, mind, and motives. May all I do be pure and acceptable in your sight and be a sweet-smelling aroma. In Jesus Name, I pray. Amen.

---

[15] Scripture quotations identified throughout this book in KJV (King James Version), NKJV (New King James Versions), NLT (New Living Translation Version), AMPC(Amplified Version Classic Edition), ESV(English Standard Version), NIV(New International Version), and NASB (New American Standard Bible) and others indicated are from www.biblegateway.com

GOD MY PROVIDER
JEHOVAH JIREH

Genesis 22:14- After God provided Abraham the Lamb for the sacrifice in place of Isaac. So, Abraham called the name of that place "The Lord will Provide" as it is to this day, **on the mount of the Lord it shall be provided (ESV).**

Scripture Application

We serve a God of all provision. The beauty of our God is that we approach Him knowing that He is all sufficient, and that He provides our every need. Hebrews 4:16 talks about the throne of grace, that we can go to it boldly when we have a need. God's provision is guaranteed. The provision may not come the way we want it to come but be assured that God will provide. How encouraging it is to approach God knowing that He will supply above and beyond what we ask for.

In daily life there supplies that may run out and need reordering. Other items may be completely out of stock, never again manufactured. Others have warrantees that expire, but God's abundant provision is guaranteed. All we need to do is ask Jehovah Jireh, who sufficiently supplies. Matthew 6:25,33 says *"Are you not of more value, your heavenly Father already knows what you need and that you need them?" 33 "But seek first the Kingdom of God and His righteousness and all these things shall be added to you"* (NKJV).

Consider this, we already have riches in heaven. Philippians 4:19 tells us: *"And my God shall supply all your need according to His riches in glory by Christ Jesus" (NKJV). Because we are children of God, and co-heirs with Christ Jesus, these riches are equally ours.* Romans 8:17 says *"Now if we are children, then we are heirs-heirs of God and co-heirs with Christ"* (NIV). This means that we have access to the heavenly storehouses, and we can ask God to release these riches to us, but first we must seek Him and His desires for us. These riches are not limited to physical or material needs, they also include emotional, relational, and spiritual needs - the Scriptures says ALL your needs. God will meet the need that is presented at the moment.

In most companies, employee's performance evaluations are scored based on merit. The ranks range from unsatisfactory, satisfactory, average, above average and exceptional. How encouraging to know that God always ranks each of as valuable, exceptional, extraordinary, uniquely gifted, important, and honorable; thus, He will not hold anything good from us (see Psalms 84:11). Jehovah Jireh continues to provide exceptionally, immeasurably more, above all we ask or think, according to the power that works within us, Halleluiah!

Scriptures of Affirmation
God will provide

- Matthew 6:25-33: Jesus teaching - do not be anxious about tomorrow, what to eat or what shall we drink or what to wear. For as the God our Father provides for the birds and clothes the grass, Are you not of more value, your heavenly Father already knows what you need and that you need them, but seek first the Kingdom of God and everything shall be added to you (NKJV).

- Hebrews 4:16: Let us therefore come boldly to the throne of grace, that we may obtain mercy and find grace to help in time of need (NKJV).

- Philippians 4:19: And my God shall supply all your need according to His riches in glory by Christ Jesus (NKJV).

- Psalm 84:11: For the Lord God is a sun and shield; The Lord will give grace and glory; No good thing will He withhold from those who walk uprightly (NKJV).

- Matthew 7:9-11: You parents—if your children ask for a loaf of bread, do you give them a stone instead? Or if they ask for a fish, do you give them a snake? Of course not! So, if you sinful people know how to give good gifts to your children, how much more will your heavenly Father give good gifts to those who ask him (NLT).

- Now unto him that is able to do exceedingly abundantly above all that we ask or think, according to the power that worketh in us" ([16]Ephesians 3:20 KJV).

Prayer

Father, in the Name of Jesus, I thank you, for provision. I thank you, that you know my needs even before I ask for them. I thank you, that as the Creator, you have abundance in your storehouses, and you know exactly when and where to extract what I need and bring it to me. I thank you, Lord, that when I ask you give me what I need, exceeding above what I asked for, or thought about. Lord, I am now bringing this supplication to you (name the needs). I ask that you release your Angels to help me

---

[16] Scripture quotations identified throughout this book in KJV (King James Version), NKJV (New King James Versions), NLT (New Living Translation Version), AMPC(Amplified Version Classic Edition), ESV(English Standard Version), NIV(New International Version), and NASB (New American Standard Bible) and others indicated are from www.biblegateway.com

gather this need. I pray that you place me in the right place, with the right people, and the right connections for this need to be met. Lord, I pray for patience to wait for the answer. I pray that you remove all ungodly desires to acquire this need in my own strength. I declare self-control, discipline, and patience for your appointed time. I bless you and thank you because you have heard me and have already provided. In Jesus Name, Amen.

GOD MY PEACE
JEHOVAH SHALOM

CHAPTER 10

Judges 6:17-24- After Gideon had made meat and unleavened bread, he brought the offering to the angel who sat under the oak tree. The angel said, "put the meat and the bread on the rock and pour the broth over it." Then the angel touched the meat and the bread with the end of the staff he was holding, and fire came out of the rock and consumed the meat and bread. Gideon realized that IT WAS THE SOVERIEGN LORD AND SAID, "I HAVE SEEN YOUR ANGEL- MY LORD JESUS CHRIST." The Lord said, "PEACE, you will not die." Gideon then built an altar there to the Lord and called it the LORD IS PEACE (NKJV).

Scripture Application

"Shalom" is a common phrase in Christian circles. I found this definition of shalom online. According to the writer, shalom is a Hebrew word taken from the root word shalam, which means "to be safe in mind, body, or estate." It speaks of completeness, fullness, or of a type of wholeness that encourages you to give back (https://firm.org.il/learn/the-meaning-of-shalom). Shalom, also, means peace-the absence of war; it involves an inward sense of completeness or wholeness.

Peace encompasses everything, our mind, soul, and body. When one aspect of our life is affected, peace is disrupted also in the unaffected parts of our life. So, the definition of peace as completeness and fullness is accurate. God our Shalom provides the ultimate peace – as humans we can be tempted to seek peace in materialism or from others, but Jehovah Shalom is our peace.

God's peace overcomes anxiety, fear, and worry. The pressures of life can cause a lot of discord, but Jesus Christ was chastised for our peace (see Isaiah 53:5). When confronted with anxiety, worry or confusion on issues, ask God to wash you with His peace. Philippians 4:6 encourages us to be anxious for nothing, but by prayer, supplication, and thanksgiving, make your requests be known to God; and the peace of God that surpasses human understanding will GUARD (protect, secure, shield) your hearts and minds through Christ Jesus.

I have also learned to be led by God's peace in decision making. Some issues can be so complex and risky, but I have learned to lean on the Holy Spirit, and to be led by peace towards a decision. Any decision that results in haste, anxiety, fear, worry, confusion, or doubt is often ungodly. I have learned to refrain from making any decisions when this happens and to seek God for direction - always waiting to be directed by His peace.

Lastly, the Lord is Peace. Having accepted Jesus as Lord and Savior, we must purpose to be carriers of His peace. Romans 12:18 says *"If it is possible, as far as it depends on you, live at peace with everyone"* (NIV). In Hebrews 12:14 we see that peace goes hand in hand with holiness; *"Pursue peace with all people, and holiness, without which no one will see the Lord"* (NKJV). Being a peacemaker in all situations can be challenging. It may require letting go of an offense when you are wrongly accused. It may require humility and refusing to engage in a conflict when one is instigated. Though tough, remember that peace seeds when sown will result in a great harvest. In James 3:18 we read that those who are *"peacemakers will plant seeds of peace and reap a harvest of righteousness"* (NLT).

Scriptures of Affirmation
I have peace

- John 14:27: Jesus saying, "My peace I leave with you, My peace I GIVE you, not as the world gives do, I give to you, let not your heart be troubled, neither let it be afraid (NKJV).

- Eph 2:14: For He Himself is our peace, Who has made both one, and has broken down the middle wall of separation (NKJV).

- Isaiah 53:5: But He was wounded for our transgressions, He was bruised for our iniquities; **the chastisement (the punishment)** for our peace was upon Him, and by His stripes we are healed. (NKJV). Christ was already punished so that we can have peace.

- Psalm 29:11: The Lord gives his people strength. The Lord blesses them with peace (NLT).

- Philippians 4:6: Be anxious for nothing, but by prayer, supplication, and thanksgiving, make your requests be known to God; and **the peace of God** that surpasses human understanding will GUARD (protect, secure, shield) your hearts and minds through Christ Jesus (NKJV).

- Colossians 3:15: And let the peace that comes from Christ rule in your hearts. For as members of one body you are called to live in peace. And always be thankful (NLT).

- Hebrews 7:1-2: For this Melchizedek, king of Salem, priest of the Most High God (Jesus Christ is our high priest now), who met Abraham returning from the slaughter of kings and blessed him. In whom Abraham gave a tenth part of all, first being translated king of righteousness and also King of Salem meaning **King of Peace** (ESV).

- Galatians 5:22-23: But the Holy Spirit produces this kind of fruit in our lives: love, joy, peace, patience, kindness, goodness, faithfulness, gentleness, and self-control. There is no law against these things (NLT).

- Proverbs 16:7: When people's lives please the Lord, even their enemies are at peace with them (NLT).

- Proverbs 12:20: Deceit fills hearts that are plotting evil; joy fills hearts that are planning peace ([17]NLT).

Prayer

Lord Jesus Christ, I thank you, as you are my peace. I receive and embrace the peace that you have given me. Lord, you were punished for my peace, and I do not have to accept anxiety, worry, torment, irritability, fear, chaos, confusion, or anything else that robs me of Your peace. I call upon you, Jesus Christ, King of Kings and Prince of Peace; I now release to you every concern related to this situation, casting all my cares upon You, because you care for me. I now release to you Lord every area of my life that needs your peace: family relationships, marriage, finances, job, business, investments, ministry, and decisions I need to make. I renounce all worry, anxiety, fear, confusion, turmoil, restlessness, anger, and irritability. I take Your peace as a shield to guard my heart and mind. Thank you, God of peace, - Jehovah Shalom- In Jesus Name, Amen!

---

[17] Scripture quotations identified throughout this book in KJV (King James Version), NKJV (New King James Versions), NLT (New Living Translation Version), AMPC(Amplified Version Classic Edition), ESV(English Standard Version), NIV(New International Version), and NASB (New American Standard Bible) and others indicated are from www.biblegateway.com

GOD MY DEFENSE
JEHOVAH SABAOTH
COMMANDER OF THE
ARMIES OF THE LORD
LORD OF HOSTS

CHAPTER 11

1 Samuel 17:45-Then David said to the Philistine, You have come to me with a sword, with a spear and with a javelin, but I come to you in the Name of the Lord of Hosts, the God of the Armies of Israel whom you defied (NKJV).

Scripture Application

We may feel defeated when we experience overwhelming situations which is often accompanied by physical, emotional, and at times, financial and spiritual exhaustion. There was a season when I was very overwhelmed by attacks of the enemy. It felt like I was in a marathon of spiritual warfare. Most of the attacks were happening to me for the first time-they were unique in their presentation – I waged war so hard, to the point of exhaustion!

I believe God allowed the attacks to train me in other aspects of spiritual warfare that I had not been exposed to; but He also taught me how to engage His heavenly hosts and His angelic army in warfare. The attacks forced me to study the roles of the heavenly hosts and the angelic in spiritual warfare, which I partially knew, but these experiences enhanced my knowledge.

I learned many lessons from these experiences, the most important one was that "God is always for you". God is always on your side, despite what the enemy will throw at you. We always war in victory and from victory NOT for victory. This warring from victory is part of our identity as believers in Christ. When we approach God with confidence in what He has created us for; when we call for help, He shows up!

First mentioned in 1 Samuel 1:3, Yahweh Sabaoth is also used to express God's great power. Lord of Hosts stands for an army, which I believe are battalions of Angels, who are specialized in war. Sabaoth is God's military might and power, who are dedicated to fight and win our battles. God's ways of fighting battles often differ from ours. So, do not fight alone. Know the support system that you have and invite them to join with you in fighting all your battles. Many more are always with you than what the enemy has (see 2 Kings 6:16-23: NKJV). We have this line-up of assistants: the Commander of the Armies of the Lord, Lord of Lords, Mighty Man of War, King of Glory, the Spirit of the Lord, Lord of Hosts, and Jehovah Sabaoth!

Scriptures of Affirmation
The Lord is my defense

- Joshua 5:13-15: Once when Joshua was by Jericho, he looked up and saw a man standing before him with a drawn sword in his hand. Joshua went to him and said to him, "Are you one of us, or one of our adversaries?" He replied, "Neither; **but as commander of the army of the Lord I have now come."** And Joshua fell on his face to the earth and worshiped, and he said to him, "What do you command your servant, my lord?" The commander of the army of the Lord said to Joshua, "Remove the sandals from your feet, for the place where you stand is holy." And Joshua did so (NRSV).

- Jeremiah 31:35: Thus, says the Lord, who gives the sun for light by day and the fixed order of the moon and the stars for light by night, who stirs up the sea so that its waves roar— **the Lord of hosts is his name** (ESV).

- 2 Kings 6:16-17: He replied, "Do not be afraid, for there are more with us than there are with them." Then Elisha prayed: "O Lord, please open his eyes that he may see." So, the Lord opened the eyes of the servant, and **he saw; the mountain was full of horses and chariots of fire all around Elisha** (NRSV).

- Psalms 91:11: For He will command his angels concerning you to guard you in all your ways (ESV).

- Exodus 15:3: The LORD is a man of war; the LORD is his name (ESV).

- Isaiah 42:13: The LORD will go forth like a warrior; He will stir up His zeal like a soldier. He will shout; yes, He will roar. He will prevail against His enemies (NIV).

- Psalm 59:5: You, Lord God of hosts, are God of Israel. Rouse yourself to punish all the nations; spare none of those who treacherously plot evil (ESV).

- 1 Samuel 1:3: Now this man used to go up year by year from his city to worship and to sacrifice to the Lord of hosts at Shiloh, where the two sons of Eli, Hophni and Phinehas, were priests of the Lord (ESV).

- Psalm 24:8-10: Who is this King of Glory? The LORD strong and mighty, the LORD mighty in battle. Who is this King of glory? The Lord of hosts, He is the King of glory (ESV).

- Zechariah 4:6: Then he said to me, "This is the word of the Lord to Zerubbabel: Not by might, nor by power, but by my Spirit, says the Lord of hosts (ESV).

- 1 Samuel 4: 4: So the people sent to Shiloh, and from there they carried the ark of the covenant of the **LORD OF HOSTS who sits above the cherubim**; and the two sons of Eli, Hophni and Phinehas, were there with the ark of the covenant of God (ESV).

- Romans 8:31-39: What then shall we say to these things? **If God is for us, who can be against us?** He who did not spare His own Son, but delivered Him up for us all, how shall He not with Him also freely give us all things? Who shall bring a charge against God's elect? It is God who justifies. Who is he who condemns? It is Christ who died, and furthermore is also risen, who is even at the right hand of God, who also makes intercession for us. *Who shall separate us from the love of Christ? Shall tribulation, or distress, or persecution, or famine, or nakedness, or peril, or sword?* As it is written: For Your sake we are killed all day long; we are accounted as sheep for the slaughter. "Yet in all these things we are more than conquerors through Him who loved us. *For I am persuaded that neither death nor life, nor angels nor principalities nor powers, nor things present nor things to come, nor height nor depth, nor any other created thing, shall be able to separate us from the love of God which is in Christ Jesus our Lord (NKJV).*

- Psalm 24:8: Who is this King of glory? The Lord strong and mighty, The Lord mighty in battle ([18]NKJV).

---

[18] Scripture quotations identified throughout this book in KJV (King James Version), NKJV (New King James Versions), NLT (New Living Translation Version), AMPC(Amplified Version Classic Edition), ESV(English Standard Version), NIV(New International Version), and NASB (New American Standard Bible) and others indicated are from www.biblegateway.com

Prayer

Lord of Hosts, I thank you, for Your Love for me. I thank you, for the heavenly hosts, and the vast armies you have in place for me. I bless You, for the wars you have endlessly fought and won for me. As for this war I am in now, I ask you Lord, that you once again engage Your armies on my behalf. I declare you, Lord Jesus, as my Commander-in-Chief as well and ask you Lord to engage and fight for me. Lord, release Your hosts to fight against principalities, powers, rulers of darkness and all forms of wickedness. Lord, I ask that you release your hosts to fight for me in all spheres of life in the atmosphere, on earth, in the heavenlies, the underworld and the waters. Lord, release Your armies to divert and destroy all attacks of the enemy that are projected, planned or are already in place. Lord of Hosts, intervene on my behalf for my life, my family, my children, my neighborhood, my city, my country, my village, my continent, my destiny, my ministry, my job, my finances, my business, and my career, in the Name of Jesus. The Lord strong in battle, thank you, Jesus, for crowning me with victory. Thank you, Lord, because I am constantly victorious in you, in Jesus Name, Amen!

GOD MY BANNER
JEHOVAH NISSI

*Exodus 17:14-16-*Then the Lord said to Moses, "Write this as a memorial in a book and recite it in the ears of Joshua, that I will utterly blot out the memory of Amalek from under heaven." And Moses built an altar and called the name of it, **The Lord Is My Banner**, saying, "A hand upon the throne of the Lord! The Lord will have war with Amalek from generation to generation" (NKJV).

Scripture Application

The LORD is my Banner. Nissi is derived from the Hebrew word nis, which means "banner." In biblical times, armies had a banner or a flag as a focus point of strength and courage to continue to war to victory. When Moses led the Israelites, the Lord was their focal point-their banner. God continues to war for us also as we put our trust in Him. Moses, Joshua, and the Israelites had major victories, triumphing over their enemies because the Lord continually fought for them. The Lord will do the same for us.

Scriptures of Affirmation
The Lord fights for me

- Exodus 14:13-14: And Moses said to the people, "Fear not, stand firm, and see the salvation of the Lord, which he will work for you today. For the Egyptians whom you see today, you shall never see again. The Lord will fight for you, and you have only to be silent (ESV).

- Psalm 24:8: Who is this King of glory? The LORD strong and mighty, the LORD mighty in battle (KJV).

- Exodus 20:3-4: And shall say to them, 'Hear, O Israel, today you are drawing near for battle against your enemies: let not your heart faint. Do not fear or panic or be in dread of them, for the Lord your God is he who goes with you to fight for you against your enemies, to give you the victory (ESV).

- Psalm 20:7: Some trust in chariots and some in horses, but we trust in the name of the Lord our God (ESV).

- Isaiah 59:19: So shall they fear the name of the Lord from the west, and His glory from the rising of the sun; When the enemy comes in like a flood, The Spirit of the Lord will lift up a standard against him (NKJV).

- Romans 8:31: What then shall we say to these things? If God is for us, who can be against us (NKJV).

- Psalm 44:4-7: You are my King and my God, who decrees victories for Jacob. Through You we push back our enemies through Your Name we trample our foes. I put no trust in my bow, my sword does not bring me victory; but You give us victory over our enemies, You put our adversaries to shame (NIV).

- Matthew 10:28: Do not be afraid of those who kill the body but cannot kill the soul. Rather, be afraid of the One who can destroy both soul and body in hell (NIV).

- Deuteronomy 20:3b-4: Do not be fainthearted or afraid; do not panic or be terrified by them. For the Lord, your God is the one who goes with you to fight for you against your enemies to give you victory (NIV).

- Joshua 1:5: No man shall be able to stand before you all the days of your life; as I was with Moses, so I will be with you (NKJV).

- Isaiah 52:1: Awake, awake! Put on your strength, O Zion; Put on your beautiful garments, O Jerusalem, the holy city! For the uncircumcised and the unclean shall no longer come to you (NKJV).

- Jeremiah 1:18-19: For behold, I have made you this day a fortified city and an iron pillar and bronze walls against the whole land— Against the kings of Judah, against its princes, against its priests, and against the people of the land. They will fight against you, but they shall not prevail against you. For I am with you," says the Lord, "to deliver you" (NKJV).

- John 10:10: The thief does not come except to steal, and to kill, and to destroy. I have come that they may have life, and that they may have it more abundantly (NKJV).

- 2 Corinthians 10:4-6: For the weapons of our warfare are not carnal but mighty in God for pulling down strongholds, casting down arguments and every high thing that exalts itself against the knowledge of God, bringing every thought into captivity to the obedience of Christ and being ready to punish all disobedience when your obedience is fulfilled (NKJV).

- 2 Corinthians 2:14: Now thanks be to God who always leads us in triumph in Christ, and through us diffuses the fragrance of His knowledge in every place ([19]NKJV).

Prayer

Father God, I thank you, for the continuous assurance of victory according to 2 Corinthians 2:14. I thank you, for the Holy Spirit who raises a standard against my enemies. I thank you, for the warring Angels that you dispatch daily to come to my rescue. I thank you, for fighting for me even when I do not see it. Lord, I come to you now concerning these conflicts and battles, I turn them over to you. Lord, engage your armies on my behalf. I partner with you and with the mighty weapons of warfare that you have given me - and Lord, I know you are on my side. I thank you for warring for me in the heavenlies, the earth, the atmosphere, the underworld, and the bottom of the seas, oceans, and all water masses. I thank you, for the wall of defense you have placed around me and my family. I thank you, Lord, for victory. I will keep my eyes fixed on you God, my banner, and Your flag of victory flies over my enemies. Thank you, Lord for Your endless, vast protection. I give you all glory, honor, and thanksgiving for Your mighty works. Thank you, Lord, Great God, Mighty in War! In Jesus Name, Amen.

---

[19] Scripture quotations identified throughout this book in KJV (King James Version), NKJV (New King James Versions), NLT (New Living Translation Version), AMPC(Amplified Version Classic Edition), ESV(English Standard Version), NIV(New International Version), and NASB (New American Standard Bible) and others indicated are from www.biblegateway.com

THE LORD OF JUSTICE, RIGHTEOUNESS AND TRUTH

Psalm 89:14- Righteousness and justice are the foundation of Your throne; Mercy and truth go before Your face (NKJV).

Scripture Application

God is just in everything He does; He shows no partiality. God does not show favoritism. He is Jehovah **Elohim, Creator and Judge**. He judges everything with equity. This is an encouraging aspect of God's attributes because we know that God will judge and respond in fairness. I have applied these attributes of God when I have petitioned him on issues relating to accusations from Satan, that need to be revoked, and also on generational hinderances, that need to be removed to obtain breakthrough.

Relational misunderstandings, false rumors, gossip, or slander can result in a lot of conflict. At times in our attempts to explain ourselves the conflict gets magnifies. It often best to let God fight such battles for you. I often declare God's attributes of justice and truth when accusations were made against me. I have asked God to expose the truth of the matter to my accusers, and to those who had judged me harshly; and I saw the Lord vindicate me every time. The Lord showed me that His vindication may not happen immediately, but with time He will vindicate and exonerate us!

The next area where these attributes can be applied is justice! Where justice is needed, we should rely on the justice of God. There are many injustices done against children, women, people of different faiths or religion, people groups and races. On issues of oppression, slavery, and captivity of such groups, we should call for the God of justice to intervene.

Remember God judges through the eyes of righteousness, justice, and truth because these are His foundations; He will never twist His laws around in favor of someone!

Scriptures of Affirmation
The Lord Vindicates me

- Psalm 97:1-6: The Lord reigns, let the earth be glad; let the distant shores rejoice. Clouds and thick darkness surround him; righteousness and justice are the foundation of his throne. Fire goes before him and consumes his foes on every side. His lightning lights up the world; the earth sees and trembles. The mountains melt like wax before the Lord before the Lord of all the earth. The heavens proclaim his righteousness and all peoples see his glory (NIV).

- Job 12:22: He uncovers deep things out of darkness and brings the shadow of death to light (NKJV).

- Proverbs 21:15: Justice is a joy to the godly, but it terrifies evildoers (NIV).

- Amos 5:24: But let justice roll on like a river, righteousness like a never-failing stream! (NIV).

- Deuteronomy 32:4-5: For I proclaim the name of the Lord: Ascribe greatness to our God. He is the Rock; His work is perfect; for all His ways are justice a God of truth and without injustice; righteous and upright is He (NKJV).

- 2 Thessalonians 1:6-8: Since it is a righteous thing with God to repay with tribulation those who trouble you and to give you who are troubled rest with us when the Lord Jesus is revealed from heaven with His mighty angels in flaming fire taking vengeance on those who do not know God, and on those who do not obey the gospel of our Lord Jesus Christ (NKJV).

- 2 Chronicles 19:7: Now let the fear of the Lord be on you. Judge carefully, for with the Lord our God there is no injustice or partiality or bribery (NIV).

- Hebrews 6:1: For God is not unjust so as to forget your work and the love which you have shown toward His name, in having ministered and in still ministering to the saints ([20]NASB).

Prayer

Father, in the Name of Jesus, I thank you, for being the God of justice, truth and righteousness. I thank you, for the many battles you have fought for me and for the victory I have in you. I bless and honor you, for your vindications, as the accuser of the brethren is already defeated. Therefore, Lord, I repent of any sin, iniquity, or transgression on my part, and also for anything I did, said or even though related to these accusations or misunderstandings and ask for Your forgiveness. Let the Blood of Jesus

---

[20] Scripture quotations identified throughout this book in KJV (King James Version), NKJV (New King James Versions), NLT (New Living Translation Version), AMPC(Amplified Version Classic Edition), ESV(English Standard Version), NIV(New International Version), and NASB (New American Standard Bible) and others indicated are from www.biblegateway.com

erase my faults. I renounce everything I could have acquired or given legal rights to in Jesus Name. I now ask Lord, for your acquittal on any case presented to You. I ask that you revoke all judgments placed upon me by the enemy and let Your justice be exercised on my behalf. Lord, vindicate me in Your truth, and righteousness. I ask for the advocacy of the Holy Spirit and the mediation of Jesus Christ. Lord, let every injunction against me be cancelled in Jesus Name. Let all the ordinances of Satan be cancelled in all areas of my life. Let the verdicts of hell be cancelled. Let your judgment stand, and your purposes concerning me be restored. Lord, release what was held back. Restore seven thousand-fold in Jesus Name. I believe that you are the God of vindication and restitution. I now gather all my spoils, I gather all that belongs to me and receive them by faith in Jesus Name, Amen.

THE LORD MY DELIVERER

CHAPTER 14

*Psalm 18:2-3-*The LORD is my rock and my fortress and my deliverer, my God, my rock, in whom I take refuge, my shield, and the horn of my salvation, my stronghold. I call upon the Lord, who is worthy to be praised, and I am saved from my enemies (NASB).

Scripture Application

God's deliverance works concurrently with His defense, salvation, healing, and protection. Born-again believers, as spiritual beings, deal with opposition from spiritual entities. These spiritual entities may use fellow human beings as well as physical means to attack the born-again believer. But praise be to God who always gives us the victory. We engage in such battles with God's help and by the power of the Holy Spirit. Although common sense, knowledge, human intelligence, rationale, logic, and physical means are important, and should be utilized, they should not be exclusively relied upon for deliverance because they are never sufficient to guarantee total deliverance, protection, and security. Total deliverance is in the Lord our God; He is our Rock, our Fortress, our Shied, the Lord our Salvation, the Lord our Stronghold!

At times we may attempt to force our deliverance by human efforts, instead of relying on God. We often want "to fix things", but spiritual matters cannot be approached through physical means. With humility, prayer, and repentance we search God's word on the issue at hand, and then through faith, and in collaboration with the Holy Spirit we engage our weapons of warfare.

Additionally, faith plays a big role in deliverance, as it does in all aspects of our walk with God. There was a season in which I was severely attacked by the enemy. The attacks were constant; I did not know the depth of spiritual warfare as I do now. I recall saying "simple prayers" and God delivered me. So, pray by faith, walk by faith; and believe in God. He has you covered as you engage in prayer, including prayers for deliverance.

God delivers us by guiding us and by keeping His eyes on us at all times. His deliverance is diverse by nature. He delivers us from evil and temptations, from impending danger, from traps and snares set by the enemy, from internal, external and supernatural factors; as well as through preservation, as He ensures that we are not exposed to places, people or things we should not be exposed to, and also through the divine protection of His Angels. This is the power of God's deliverance. Scriptures that encapsulate aspects of God's deliverance are found in Psalm 91 and 2 Samuel 22. Continue to dwell in the Shadow of the Almighty and watch Him encircle you with deliverance, over your life and future generations.

Scriptures of Affirmation
My God shall deliver me

- Psalm 32:7: You are my hiding place; You preserve me from trouble; You surround me with songs of deliverance. Selah (ESV).

- 2 Chronicles 20:17: You need not fight in this battle; station yourselves, stand and see the salvation of the LORD on your behalf, O Judah and Jerusalem 'Do not fear or be dismayed; tomorrow go out to face them, for the LORD is with you (ESV).

- Psalm 140:7: O Lord, my Lord, the strength of my salvation, you have covered my head in the day of battle. (ESV).

- 2 Kings 19:19: So now, O Lord our God, save us, please, from his hand, that all the kingdoms of the earth may know that you, O Lord, are God alone" (ESV).

- Obadiah 1:17 But on Mount Zion there will be those who escape, and it will be holy, and the house of Jacob will possess their possessions (ESV).

- Psalm 74:12-17: For God is my King from of old, **working salvation in the midst of the earth**. You divided the sea by Your strength; You broke the heads of the sea serpents in the waters. You broke the heads of Leviathan in pieces and gave him as food to the people inhabiting the wilderness. You broke open the fountain and the flood; You dried up mighty rivers. The day is Yours; the night also is Yours; You have prepared the light and the sun. You have set all the borders of the earth; You have made summer and winter (NKJV).

- Psalm 3:8: Salvation belongs to the LORD; Your blessing be upon Your people! Selah (ESV).

- Psalm 42:8: The LORD will command His lovingkindness in the daytime; And His song will be with me in the night, A prayer to the God of my life (ESV).

- Psalm 34:4-7: I sought the Lord, and He heard me and delivered me from all my fears. They looked to Him and were radiant and their faces were not ashamed. This poor man cried out, and the Lord heard him and saved him out of all his troubles. The angel of the Lord encamps all around those who fear Him and delivers them (NKJV).

- Psalm 107:6-9: Then they cried out to the Lord in their trouble and He delivered them out of their distresses and He led them forth by the right way, that they might go to a city for a dwelling place .Oh, that men would give thanks to the Lord for His goodness, and for His wonderful works to the children of men! For He satisfies the longing soul and fills the hungry soul with goodness (NKJV).

- Psalm 121 6-8: The Lord is your keeper; the Lord is your shade at your right hand. The sun shall not strike you by day, nor the moon by night. The Lord shall preserve you from all evil; He shall preserve your soul. The Lord shall preserve you are going out and your coming in from this time forth and even forevermore ([21]NKJV).

Prayer

Father, I come to you in the Name of Jesus Christ, and through the blood that Jesus shed on the cross. I thank you, for your promises that those who run to you and call on you shall be delivered. Lord, you are my deliverer, I seek no other means of deliverance but yours. Father, I pray that you deliver me from every oppression of my mind, emotions, soul, and body. I pray that you deliver me from attacks of the enemy. I pray for deliverance from evil generational patterns, habits, or rituals - I break their hold off me in the name of Jesus. I pray for deliverance from any trap or snare of the enemy. Lord divert the plans and disarm the plots. Lord, I declare that you are my shield and my hiding place. I purpose to continually dwell under your shadow. Lord, I trust you; you are my hiding place; You preserve me from trouble; You shall surround me with songs of deliverance; for this I am grateful. Thank you, Lord, Amen!

---

[21] Scripture quotations identified throughout this book in KJV (King James Version), NKJV (New King James Versions), NLT (New Living Translation Version), AMPC(Amplified Version Classic Edition), ESV(English Standard Version), NIV(New International Version), and NASB (New American Standard Bible) and others indicated are from www.biblegateway.com

THE LORD MY SHEPHERD
JEHOVAH ROI

Genesis 49:24- But his bow remained in strength, And the arms of his hands were made strong by the hands of the Mighty God of Jacob; from there is **The Shepherd, the Stone of Israel** (NKJV).

John 10:14- **I am the good Shepherd;** and I know My sheep and I am known by My own (NKJV).

Scripture Application

In the natural, a shepherd has many roles. A responsible shepherd not only ensures that the flock gets good pastures, but he/she also protects, guides, and ensures that the flock is well sheltered. God epitomizes the true role of the Shepherd.

For provision, the Lord assures us that *"He will provide all of our needs according to His riches in glory"* (see Philippians 4:19, NKJV). *"The righteous never lack any good thing"* according to Psalms 84:11. *"In Him there is exceedingly abundantly above all that we ask or think"* (see Ephesians 3:20; NKJV). When we ask, He provides. Psalm 2:8 says, *"Ask me, and I will make the nations your inheritance, the ends of the earth your possession (ESV)."*

The Lord is a great protector. He shields us with His love. He has angels assigned to minister to us on a regular basis. He says His eyes are always upon us. Psalm 34:15 tells us that *"The eyes of the Lord are upon the righteous, and his ears are open unto their cry" (KJV)*. When we inhabit His shelter, we are protected by His shadow, and covered with His feathers under His wings (see Psalm:91, NKJV). Under God's protection we are preserved from diseases, demonic attacks, temptation, and natural disasters. The Lord's protection brings peace, security, and prosperity (see Jeremiah 33:6. NKJV). The Lord's protection is long-term, His covenant with us extends to our children and future generations.

The Lord nurtures us by ensuring that we are in environments where we are well fed. He connects us with people who can support our destinies and callings in life. He nurtures us through His word, through the Holy Spirit and through fellowship, when we invite Him. Psalm 1:3 tells us of His assuring promises of fruitfulness, growth and flourishing for the righteous, *"And he shall be like a tree firmly planted and tended by the streams of water, ready to bring forth its fruit in its season; its leaf also shall not fade or wither; and everything he does shall prosper and come to maturity"* (AMPC).

The Lord shepherds us by guiding us. A good shepherd never leads his flock astray. We, as the flock, can be assured of God's guidance. Psalm 32:8 says "I [the Lord] will instruct you and teach you in the way you should go; I will counsel you with My eye upon you" (AMPC). Through the Holy Spirit, He also trains us to discern and know His voice, enabling us to avoid deception from false voices. In John 10:5, He says, "Very truly I tell you Pharisees, anyone who does not enter the sheep pen by the gate, but climbs in by some other way, is a thief and a robber. The one who enters by the gate is the shepherd of the sheep. The gatekeeper opens the gate for him, and the sheep listen to his voice. He calls his own sheep by name and leads them out. When he has brought out all his own, he goes on ahead of them, and his sheep follow him because they know his voice. But they will never follow a stranger; in fact, they will run away from him because they do not recognize a stranger's voice" (NIV).

Scriptures of Affirmation
The Lord watches over me

- Psalm 23: **The Lord is my shepherd;** I shall not want. He makes me to lie down in green pastures; **He leads me** beside the still waters. He restores my soul; He leads me in **the paths of righteousness** For His name's sake. Yea, though I walk through the valley of the shadow of death, I will fear no evil; For You are with me; Your rod and Your staff, they comfort me. You prepare a table before me in the presence of my enemies; You anoint my head with oil; My cup runs over. Surely goodness and mercy shall follow me All the days of my life; And I will dwell in the house of the Lord forever (NKJV).

- Psalm 16:11: You will show me the path of life; In Your presence is fullness of joy; At Your right hand are pleasures forevermore (NKJV). **God will show me the path of life.**

- Psalm 32:8: I will instruct you and teach you in the way you should go; I will guide you with My eye (NKJV). He will **guide me** with His eye.

- Psalm 73:23-24: Nevertheless, **I am continually with You;** You **have taken hold of my right** hand. With Your counsel You will guide me, and afterward receive me to glory (NASB).

- Psalm 119:35: Make me walk in the path of Your commandments, For I delight in it (ESV).

- Psalm 37:23-24: The steps of a good man are ordered by the Lord, And He delights in his way. Though he falls, he shall not be utterly cast down; For the Lord upholds him with His hand. My steps are ordered by the Lord (NKJV).

- Proverbs 3:5-6: I trust in the Lord with all my heart and lean not on my own understanding. In all my ways I acknowledge Him, and He directs my paths (NIV).

- Isaiah 48:17: Thus, says the Lord, your Redeemer, the Holy One of Israel: "I am the Lord your God, who teaches you to profit, **who leads you by the way you should go**" (NASB).

- John 16:13-15: However, when He, the Spirit of truth, has come, **He will guide you into all truth**; for He will not speak on His own authority, **but whatever He hears He will speak; and He will tell you things to come.** He will glorify Me, for He will take of what is Mine and declare it to you. All things that the Father has are Mine. Therefore, I said that He [will take of Mine and declare it to you. The Spirit of truth has come, and He is guiding me into all truth. He will tell me things to come (NKJV).

- Romans 8:14: For as many as are led by the Spirit of God, these are sons of God ([22]NKJV). I am led by the Spirit of God for I a son or daughter of God.

Prayer

Thank you, Lord Jesus, for being my Shepherd. I submit to your guidance and leadership. I submit to the guidance of the Holy Spirit. I commit my ways to you and am thankful that you establish them. I pray that you make any crooked ways straight. Expose and remove all blockages in my

---

[22] Scripture quotations identified throughout this book in KJV (King James Version), NKJV (New King James Versions), NLT (New Living Translation Version), AMPC(Amplified Version Classic Edition), ESV(English Standard Version), NIV(New International Version), and NASB (New American Standard Bible) and others indicated are from www.biblegateway.com

path and break all strongholds and hinderances in my mind. Lord, expose all areas of deceit in my life. Shine Your light on the truth I need to know concerning my destiny. Lord, release Your Angels, Your Glory and Your Fire to go before me and also to be my rear guard. Lord, you know the plans you have for me. Help me walk in the fulfillment of those plans, on time, per your schedule. Lord, as you guide me, let me know your heartbeat. Help me walk in synchrony with you, never missing a step. Lord, show me what I need to do daily and how I need to do it. Bring appropriate people, resources, and support to accomplish what You want me to accomplish, daily. Lord, sustain me with Your strength to be effective and to finish well at all times. Help me finish strong. Help me finish the race and obtain a crown, in Jesus Name, Amen.

GOD MY RIGHTEOUNESS JEHOVAH TSIDKENU

Jeremiah 33:16- In those days Judah shall be saved, and Jerusalem shall dwell safely. And this is the name by which it will be called, The LORD IS OUR RIGHTEOUNESS Lord is Our Righteousness (our Rightness, our Justice) (AMPC).

Scripture Application

Righteousness means being in right standing with God. When we accepted Jesus Christ as Lord and Savior, through confession and repentance, we were reconciled to God. The sacrifice that Jesus endured, by offering Himself, restored the covenant that we once had with God.

Jehovah Tsidkenu, God my righteousness, has been extremely helpful when I struggle with guilt and shame. There are life experiences that we often regret, particularly if they resulted in hefty consequences. At times, the devil may tempt us by reminding us of the past, especially when we see the consequences, this may result in guilt and shame. At such times I am reminded of being made righteous by God and renounce the guilt and shame. When the Lord restores, He reconciles us in peace, safety, security, prosperity, and righteousness. The past is the past, and we must move into the new things that God is doing.

The other aspect of the power of our righteousness in God is when He exposes things that need to purge from us. The blood of Jesus, the Word of God, and the fire of God are all instrumental in purging us. This is God's love at such a deep level. God is a good Father, supplying us with all that we need to stay in communion with Him.

Scriptures of Affirmation
I am accepted by God

- Romans 3:21-22: But now the righteousness of God has been manifested apart from the law, although the Law and the Prophets bear witness to it— the righteousness of God through faith in Jesus Christ for all who believe (ESV).

- Romans 5:17: For if by the one man's offense death reigned through the one, much more those who receive abundance of grace and of the gift of righteousness will reign in life through the One, Jesus Christ (NKJV).

- 2 Corinthians 5:21: For our sake he made him to be sin who knew no sin, so that in him we might become the righteousness of God (ESV).

- 1 Corinthians 1:30: And because of him you are in Christ Jesus, who became to us wisdom from God, righteousness and sanctification and redemption (ESV).

- Isaiah 51:6: Lift up your eyes to the heavens, look at the earth beneath; the heavens will vanish like smoke, the earth will wear out like a garment and its inhabitants die like flies. But my salvation will last forever, my righteousness will never fail (NIV).

- Isaiah 61:10: I will greatly rejoice in the Lord, my soul will exult in my God; for He has clothed me with the garments of salvation, He has covered me with the robe of righteousness, as a bridegroom decks himself with a garland, and as a bride adorns herself with her jewels ([23]AMP).

Prayer

Lord, I thank you, for the Gift of Salvation. I thank you, that through the shed blood of Jesus I have access to you. I confess and repent of any sin, transgression, or iniquity I may have committed by action, thought, word, disobedience, rebellion, selfishness, or idolatry. I thank you, that when I repent you forgive me and forget my sins. I now receive your forgiveness and accept the robe of righteousness and garments of salvation. I consecrate all areas of my life and everything I have to you; through the blood of Jesus they are holy. I declare every part of my body, house, family, business, gifts, skills, and money as holy and righteous through the blood of Jesus. I receive salvation, healing, deliverance, and breakthrough in all areas of my life. According to your word it is finished (see Isaiah 53 and John 19). Through you I now live without guilt and condemnation. I walk in the fullness of my salvation in righteousness, peace, and joy in the Holy Spirit, in the Name of Jesus, Amen.

---

[23] Scripture quotations identified throughout this book in KJV (King James Version), NKJV (New King James Versions), NLT (New Living Translation Version), AMPC(Amplified Version Classic Edition),AMP, (Amplified Bible), ESV(English Standard Version), NIV(New International Version), and NASB (New American Standard Bible) and others indicated are from www.biblegateway.com

GOD MY SANCTIFIER
JEHOVAH M'KADDESH

Exodus 31:13- Speak also to the children of Israel, saying: Surely My Sabbaths you shall keep, for it is a sign between Me and you throughout your generations, that you may know that I am the LORD WHO SANCTIFIES YOU (NKJV).

Scripture Application

Sanctify means sanctuary or hallow, to set apart to make holy. The Lord who makes you holy. We were made holy by the blood of Jesus Christ when we accepted Him as Lord of our lives. Now, since we have been made holy, we have to maintain a lifestyle of holiness. 1 Peter 1:15 (ESV) instructs us to be holy because God is holy. Since we have received our new identity in Jesus, and we are holy we must refrain from doing anything that would defile us. Hebrews 12:14(ESV) warns that without holiness we cannot see God.

After receiving Jesus Christ, the Holy Spirit continues the work of Sanctification as He convicts us of the Word of God. John 17:17 says *"Sanctify them in the truth; your word is truth (NKJV)."* Since we have been separated unto the Lord, which is sanctification, our role then is to accept the convictions of the Holy Spirit and repent of any wrongdoing immediately. Do not ignore His convictions and continue to sin. I John 1:8-10 says *"If we say that we have no sin, we deceive ourselves, and the truth is not in us. If we confess our sins, He is faithful and just to forgive us our sins and to cleanse us from all unrighteousness. If we say that we have not sinned, we make Him a liar, and His word is not in us"* (NKJV).

Holiness is a lifestyle. It involves internal and external sanctification. By this I mean our motives, words, thoughts, and actions must be holy. This does not require being fixated on one's character, but rather being conscious of our identity as born-again Christians, and having a repentant heart, not one that is hardened towards God. The beauty of having a repentant heart is knowing that God is available at all times to forgive our sins when we repent. God is always ready to wash us as white as snow and restore us to our identity as holy children before Him. *"But you are a chosen generation, a royal priesthood, a holy nation, His own special people, that you may proclaim the praises of Him who called you out of darkness into His marvelous light; who once were not a people but are now the people of God, who had not obtained mercy but now have obtained mercy "*(1 Peter 2:9-10 (NKJV).

If holiness is a lifestyle then it involves everything in one's life. Make a habit of consecrating everything that you have as holy unto the Lord. Consecrate your house, possessions, furniture, any article that you own, your marriage, children, even your spouse. By consecrating everything to the Lord, it serves as a mark or boundary. A declaration of alertness that buffers any defiling agent from coming close. This consecration also creates an atmosphere where God can inhabit because God's dwellings are holy.

This attribute of God is also powerful in defusing thoughts of guilt and condemnation. Following repentance, whenever confronted with thoughts of past failures or sins, remind the devil that you have been sanctified, you are holy and set apart for God.

Scriptures of Affirmation:
I am God's pure vessel

- Leviticus 20:7-8: Consecrate yourselves therefore, and be holy, for I am the Lord your God. 8 And you shall keep My statutes and perform them: I am the Lord who sanctifies you (NKJV).

- Hebrews 10:9-10: Then He said, "Behold, I have come to do Your will, O God." He takes away the first that He may establish the second. By that will we have been sanctified through the offering of the body of Jesus Christ once for all (NJKV).

- John 17: 16-19: They are not of the world, even as I am not of it. Sanctify them by the truth; your word is truth. As you sent me into the world, I have sent them into the world. For them I sanctify myself, that they too may be truly sanctified (NIV.)

- 1 Corinthians 1:30: And because of him you are in Christ Jesus, who became to us wisdom from God, righteousness and sanctification and redemption (ESV).

- Ephesians 5:25-27: Husbands, love your wives, just as Christ loved the church and gave himself up for her to make her holy, cleansing her by the washing with water through the word, and to present her to himself as a radiant church, without stain or wrinkle or any other blemish, but holy and blameless (NIV).

- 1 Thessalonians 5:23-24: Now may the God of peace Himself sanctify you completely; and may your whole spirit, soul, and body be preserved blameless at the coming of our Lord Jesus Christ. He who calls you is faithful, who also will do it (NKJV).

- 1 Peter 2:9-10: But you are a chosen generation, a royal priesthood, a holy nation, His own special people, that you may proclaim the praises of Him who called you out of darkness into His marvelous light; who once were not a people but are now the people of God, who had not obtained mercy but now have obtained mercy ([24]NKJV).

Prayer

Father God, I thank you, that you are the God who sanctifies me. Thank you, for the Blood of Jesus that atoned for my sins. By the Blood of Jesus, I am redeemed from the hand of the devil, according to Ephesians 1:7 "Because of the Blood of Jesus all my SINS are forgiven." The power of sin has been broken; sin has no power over me because of the Blood of Jesus. Jesus who loved me and gave himself for me tells me in Galatians 2:20 that "I have been crucified with Christ. It is no longer I who live, but Christ who lives in me." Lord, I embrace the truth of your Word to continually sanctify me, as I read it, obey it, and apply it to my life. Lord, I submit my spirit, mind, soul, and body to your sanctification, that I may be preserved blameless before you. Lord, create in me a clean heart, expose all areas of my life that need sanctification. The Blood of Jesus Christ, the Son of God, continually cleanses me of all sin (see 1John 1:7). Through the Blood of Jesus, I am justified, made just, as if I had never sinned (see Romans 5:9). Through the Blood of Jesus, I am sanctified, and set apart for God (see Hebrews 13:12). My Body is a temple of the Holy Spirit, redeemed, and cleansed by the blood of Jesus (see [25]1 Corinthians 6:19). Because of the Blood of Jesus, Satan has no place in me, and Satan has no power over me. I have been crucified with Christ; the life I now live in the flesh that I live by the faith of Christ. I am filled and led by the Holy Spirit in the Name of Jesus Christ, Amen!

---

[24] Scripture quotations identified throughout this book in KJV (King James Version), NKJV (New King James Versions), NLT (New Living Translation Version), AMPC(Amplified Version Classic Edition),AMP, (Amplified Bible), ESV(English Standard Version), NIV(New International Version), and NASB (New American Standard Bible) and others indicated are from www.biblegateway.com

[25] Scripture quotations identified throughout this book in KJV (King James Version), NKJV (New King James Versions), NLT (New Living Translation Version), AMPC(Amplified Version Classic Edition),AMP, (Amplified Bible), ESV(English Standard Version), NIV(New International Version), and NASB (New American Standard Bible) and others indicated are from www.biblegateway.com

THE LORD IS THERE
JEHOVAH SHAMMAH
THE OMNIPRESENT GOD

CHAPTER 18

*Ezekiel 48:35-*All the way around shall be eighteen thousand cubits; and the name of the city from that day shall be: THE LORD IS THERE (NKJV).

Scripture Application

The Omnipresent nature of God is very assuring because by it, God guarantees to be present wherever we are and in every circumstance. "Well," one may ask, "how about the hard times in life? How about when I faced atrocities from fellow humans? Where was God? Why didn't He prevent what was happening or rescue me from harm?" Frankly, these are sincere questions that only God can answer. But I believe that He never left us in those moments, that He still shielded us and preserved us in some way.

I have faced some tough times from childhood to adulthood. Many times, I felt helpless, because I had no one to confide in for help, but deep inside I developed this inner strength to overcome. I believe this inner strength was from the Lord, nudging me to stay strong and keep moving. I have countless testimonies of God rescuing me from the hand of the enemy when I thought I was alone. I also have countless testimonies of God's vindication of me when false accusations came against me; as well as God's intervention, right in time, of needs for myself and for my family. I can testify of God's comfort and assurance when I was lonely, and God's deliverance, privately, when I was severely depressed and suicidal. God is always there!

I do a lot of reflective reminders of the things God has brought me through in the past. In reviewing those accounts, I can still point out saying; "Lord, I saw you in that, You were there; I saw You there too". I have countless situations to point at seeing the favor and hand of God. As you pray, know that God is there with you, and He will be there for each situation you are seeking Him for. God may bring you the answer differently that you wanted but know that He is there!

How about you step into every situation knowing that God is already there!

Scriptures of Affirmation
I am never alone

- Revelation 21:3: And I heard a loud voice from heaven saying, Behold, the tabernacle of God is with men, and He will dwell with them, and they shall be His people. God Himself will be with them and be their God (NKJV).

- Matthew 1:23: Behold, a virgin shall be with child and shall bring forth a Son, and they shall call His name Emmanuel (which being interpreted is, "God with us"). Behold, the virgin shall be with child, and shall bring forth a son, and they shall call his name Immanuel, which is, being interpreted, God with us (ESV).

- Genesis 28:15: Behold, I am with you and will keep you wherever you go and will bring you back to this land. For I will not leave you until I have done what I have promised you. (ESV).

- Joshua 1:5: No man shall be able to stand before you all the days of your life. Just as I was with Moses, so I will be with you. I will not leave you or forsake you (ESV).

- Isaiah 43:1-2: But now thus says the Lord, he who created you, O Jacob, he who formed you, O Israel: Fear not, for I have redeemed you; I have called you by name, you are mine. When you pass through the waters, I will be with you; and through the rivers, they shall not overwhelm you; when you walk through fire you shall not be burned, and the flame shall not consume you (ESV).

- Proverbs 15:3: The eyes of the LORD are in every place, Watching the evil and the good (NKJV).

- Matthew 18:20: For where two or three are gathered together in my name, there am I in the midst of them (KJV).

- Matthew 28:20: Go therefore and make disciples of all nations, baptizing them in the name of the Father and of the Son and of the Holy Spirit, 20 teaching them to observe all that I have commanded you. And behold, I am with you always, to the end of the age ([26]ESV).

---

[26] Scripture quotations identified throughout this book in KJV (King James Version), NKJV (New King James Versions), NLT (New Living Translation Version), AMPC(Amplified Version Classic Edition),AMP, (Amplified Bible), ESV(English Standard Version), NIV(New International Version), and NASB (New American Standard Bible) and others indicated are from www.biblegateway.com

Prayer

Father God, I thank you, for being there whenever I have needed you. I thank you, for being present at all times, that in you I am never alone. I thank you, for your eye that watches over me. I thank you, for the seven spirits of the Lord that go to and from across the earth. Thank you, for your presence; even when I do not feel you or see you, I know You are there. Thank you, for your hand that has held me in the past, and your hand that continues to hold me now as I go through current situations. Thank you, for watching over your words (promises, prophesies) to ensure that they come to pass. Father God expose anything that would remove Your Spirit from me. Show me anything that grieves your Spirit and would remove your presence from me- (repent of what God shows you, repent of iniquities, sins, or transgressions). Father baptize me with the Holy Spirit and with Fire again, in the Name of Jesus. Amen.

GOD MY HEALER
JEHOVAH RAPHA
YAHWEH ROFE'EKHA

Exodus 15: 24-26- And the people complained against Moses, saying, "What shall we drink?" So, he cried out to the Lord, and the Lord showed him a tree. When he cast it into the waters, the waters were made sweet. There He made a statute and an ordinance for them, and there He tested them, and said, "If you diligently heed the voice of the Lord your God and do what is right in His sight, give ear to His commandments and keep all His statutes, I will put none of the diseases on you which I have brought on the Egyptians. **For I am the Lord who heals you** (ESV).

Scripture Application

Healing is part of the salvation package when we accepted Jesus Christ as Lord and Savior. In fact, the crucifixion of Jesus and His resurrection, the entire process of what He endured from the time He was arrested to His resurrection, was to bring us salvation, healing, and restitution. It is true that Jesus finished all at the cross when He said, "IT IS FINISHED!" John 19:30 (NKJV)!

Isaiah 53:5 tells us that Jesus was chastised for our peace and by His stripes we are healed. This healing is for physical, emotional, psychological, and mental healing. There is no condition God cannot heal! Jesus took our infirmities and bore our sicknesses. Infirmities are chronic or hereditary conditions; these too can be cured by Jesus. Psalm 103 says that God redeems us from lives of destruction (ESV), so any traumatic conditions or destructive habits can be healed!

The chastisement that Jesus Christ endured was for emotional and mental healing. You can imagine Jesus being falsely accused, being insulted, spat on, belittled, abandoned, and rejected by His own disciples; above all being tortured by the same people He came to save. Jesus took on this desecration for our mental and emotional healing.

Mark 16:18 says *"They* (meaning anyone who believes in Jesus Christ) *will lay hands on the sick, and they will recover (NKJV)."* So, do not hesitate to pray for your own healing or for the healing of others.

Scriptures of Affirmation: I am Healthy and Whole

- Isaiah 53:5: But He was wounded for our transgressions, He was bruised for our iniquities; The chastisement for our peace was upon Him, and by His stripes we are healed (NKJV).

- Matt 8:16-17: When evening had come, they brought to Him many who were demon-possessed and He cast out the spirits with a word, and healed all who were sick, that it might be fulfilled which was spoken by Isaiah the prophet, saying: He Himself took our infirmities and bore our sicknesses (NKJV).

- Psalm 91:9-10: Because you have made the Lord your dwelling place-the Most High, who is my refuge no evil shall be allowed to befall you, no plague come near your tent (ESV).

- Psalm 103:1-4: Bless the Lord, O my soul; and all that is within me, bless His holy name! Bless the Lord, O my soul and forget not all His benefits: Who forgives all your iniquities, who heals all your diseases, who redeems your life from destruction, who crowns you with lovingkindness and tender mercies (NKJV).

- Mark 16:17-18: And these signs will follow those who believe: In My name they will cast out demons; they will speak with new tongues; they will take up serpents; and if they drink anything deadly, it will by no means hurt them; they will lay hands on the sick, and they will recover (NJKV).

- Psalm 107:19-20: Then they cried to the Lord in their trouble, and he delivered them from their distress. He sent out his word and healed them and delivered them from their destruction (ESV).

- Jeremiah 30:17: For I will restore health to you, and your wounds I will heal, declares the Lord, because they have called you an outcast: It is Zion, for whom no one cares (ESV).

- James 5:13-16: Is anyone among you suffering? Let him pray. Is anyone cheerful? Let him sing praise. Is anyone among you sick? Let him call for the elders of the church, and let them pray over him, anointing him with oil in the name of the Lord. And the prayer of faith will save the one who is sick, and the Lord will raise him up. And if he has committed sins, he will be forgiven. Therefore, confess your sins to one another and pray for one another, that you may be healed. The prayer of a righteous person has great power as it is working ([27]ESV).

Prayer for Physical Healing

Jehovah God, I acknowledge you as the Lord who heals me. I bless and worship you as no condition is untreatable with you. Lord Jesus, I thank you, for the finished work of the Cross. That by your stripes I AM HEALED. I therefore receive my healing right now. Father God forgive me if this sickness is tied to a sin I committed or generational iniquity or transgression. I repent Lord and ask for your forgiveness. I also repent of unforgiveness, bitterness, jealousy, anger, rage, and resentment. I ask that you forgive me for these. In Jesus Name, I renounce unforgiveness, bitterness, jealousy, anger, rage, and resentment. I command strongholds and curses associated with them to be broken. I command demons tied to them to get out of my body, soul, spirit, mind, and heart. In the authority of the Name of Jesus, and by the blood of Jesus, I command sickness and infirmity out of my body (name the sickness, name the area that is affected). I declare this area (name the areas) and my entire body, mind and spirit is healed in Jesus Name. I receive my healing. Thank you, Lord, for healing me in Jesus Name. Amen!

[27] Scripture quotations identified throughout this book in KJV (King James Version), NKJV (New King James Versions), NLT (New Living Translation Version), AMPC(Amplified Version Classic Edition),AMP, (Amplified Bible), ESV(English Standard Version), NIV(New International Version), and NASB (New American Standard Bible) and others indicated are from www.biblegateway.com

Prayer for Healing Past Wounds and Hurts Prayer for Psychological-Emotional and Mental Healing

Jehovah God, I thank you, for sending your Son Jesus Christ for my redemption. I thank you, for the Blood of Jesus that cleanses me from all sin, iniquities, hurts and pain. I appropriate that blood to receive Your forgiveness Lord. I now forgive everyone who has ever hurt me. I forgive (name the person) for hurting me (name the area of hurt). I forgive them and release them to You Lord. I renounce the pain of (name the pain or feeling) and cast it out of my mind, spirit, body, and soul. I break any covenant and soul ties associated with this hurt (name the hurt) in Jesus Name. I cancel the effects of this hurt (name of the hurt) in my life.

In the name of Jesus, I free myself from any bondage, prison, and captivity that is tied to these hurts. I break off every demonic spirit that is attached to my mind, soul, body, spirit, and heart. I subdue their powers and command them to get out in the Name of Jesus. Lord, I release your blood over every area of my life that was affected by these hurts. In the name of Jesus, I speak life, and receive joy, strength, healing, clarity, peace of mind, focus, concentration, and the ability to work and function, because in You Jesus I live, move, and have my being. Lord, refresh all my gifts and skills. I ask Holy Spirit that you fill all areas once occupied with hurt with your joy, your peace, and your strength. Lord Jesus, I receive Your mind; and I put on my clothes of righteousness. I declare that I am now one with You. I declare progress and breakthrough. I declare that I shall live in the fullness of your abundance, like an oak tree. I declare that I shall fulfill my destiny because Your oil is upon me. In Jesus Name, Amen.

THE LORD WHO HAS THE KEYS TO OPEN AND TO SHUT

CHAPTER 20

Isaiah 22:21-22- And I will clothe him with your tunic and tie your sash securely about him. I will entrust him with your authority and he will become a father to the inhabitants of Jerusalem and to the house of Judah .Then I will set the key of the house of David on his shoulder, When he opens no one will shut, When he shuts no one will open. I will drive him like a peg in a firm place and he will become a throne of glory to his father's house (NASB).

Scripture Application

Keys give or deny access to things. These keys apply to opening or restricting doors of destiny. Jesus Christ is the door keeper - in Revelation 3:20 He says, *"I stand at the door." In the gospel of John, He teaches that no one can come to God except by Him (NKJV), also see* John 10:9;NKJV)

Per Jeremiah 29:11, God already established a plan for each of us before we were born. That same God has the keys to open doors that are related to those plans. As part of our destiny and in order to lead, there are certain areas of influence that we need, and keys are necessary to access these areas. So, we need to pursue these doors of destiny in order to fully function and maximize our potential. This requires seeking the One with keys to open the necessary doors for you. God will open these doors as we mature from one stage to another.

Therefore, I encourage you to reflect on your life and destiny, and about doors that need to be opened and doors that need to be closed. Pray to the One who has the keys to open and shut what is needed. Also, consider this, Jesus has already granted you keys. He says in Matthew 16:19: *"I will give you the keys of the kingdom of heaven; and whatever you bind on earth shall have been bound in heaven, and whatever you loose on earth shall have been loosed in heaven"* (NASB). Use the authority and power God has given you to open the doors that need to be opened and shut the doors that are not necessary.

Scriptures of Affirmation
I have limitless potential

- Revelation 3:7: And to the angel of the church in Philadelphia write, "These things says He who is holy, He who is true, He who has the key of David, He who opens, and no one shuts, and shuts and no one opens" (NKJV).

- Matthew 16:18-19: I also say to you that you are Peter, and upon this rock I will build My church; and the gates of Hades will not overpower it. I will give you the keys of the kingdom of heaven; and whatever you bind on earth shall have been bound in heaven, and whatever you loose on earth shall have been loosed in heaven (NASB).

- Revelation 3:18: I know your works. See, I have set before you an open door, and no one can shut it; for you have a little strength, have kept My word, and have not denied My name (NKJV).

- Psalm 24:7-10: Lift up your heads, O you gates! And be lifted up, you everlasting doors! And the King of glory shall come in. Who is this King of glory? The Lord strong and mighty, The Lord mighty in battle. Lift up your heads, O your gates! Lift up, you everlasting doors! And the King of glory shall come in who is this King of glory The Lord of hosts, He is the King of glory. Selah (NKJV).

- Psalm 78:23-28: Yet he gave a command to the skies above and opened the doors of the heavens; he rained down manna for the people to eat, he gave them the grain of heaven. Human beings ate the bread of angels; he sent them all the food they could eat. He let loose the east wind from the heavens and by his power made the south wind blow. He rained meat down on them like dust, birds like sand on the seashore. He made them come down inside their camp, all around their tents (NIV).

- Nahum 1:9: Whatever they plot against the Lord He will end; trouble will not come a second time ([28]NIV).

Prayer

Father, in the Name of Jesus, I thank you, for the plans you have already outlined for my life. I thank you, for leading me thus far. Lord, I agree with you as the Lord who has keys to open and shut. I pray Lord, that you show me the doors I need to access and the ones I need to shut. Lord, I pray that you open all doors that are related to my destiny, doors of the past, present and future. In the authority and power that you have given me, I shut all doors and gateways that are unrelated to my destiny, in the Name of Jesus. I open doors and gateways that are related to my destiny in Jesus Name. I give you praise and thank you as I lift up my gates for your glory to come in. In Jesus Name Amen.

---

[28] Scripture quotations identified throughout this book in KJV (King James Version), NKJV (New King James Versions), NLT (New Living Translation Version), AMPC(Amplified Version Classic Edition),AMP, (Amplified Bible), ESV(English Standard Version), NIV(New International Version), and NASB (New American Standard Bible) and others indicated are from www.biblegateway.com

THE ALPHA AND OMEGA THE GOD OF PERFECT TIMING

CHAPTER 21

Revelation 1:8 – "I am the Alpha and the Omega, the Beginning and the End," says the Lord, "who is and who was and who is to come, the Almighty" (NKJV).

Scripture Application

I often reflect on this aspect of God when I get restless and anxious about prayers that have not been answered. I find hope and assurance in knowing that God sees the end from the beginning, and that He has already planned for all things to occur in His perfect timing. The seasons of waiting are the most challenging seasons; especially when you feel you have exhausted all you need to do about the matter. But God is faithful to bring to pass what He promised you, just in time. 2 Corinthians 1:20 says that all of God's promises are yes and amen to those who trust Him; and Jeremiah 1:12 says that God watches over His word to perform it; what He said or planned must happen. God does not speak empty words; His words are active, and they must produce what they were sent to do.

The aspect of God as the Alpha and Omega is that He is in charge of all things. When God instructs us to do something, we as humans, may not see the end product of what He is doing. Initially when we embark on such projects, we may not know what God is up to. The goal is to stay the course, trust God and know that He will bring us to a perfect end. There is hope that He who started a good work in us will bring it to completion (see Philippians 1:6; NKJV).

Regardless of where you are right now, trust God in the journey. Know that the Alpha and Omega is never too early or too late. Certainly, we can pray for Him to hasten some things in our favor but remember that God is always on time - His timing is perfect. Habakkuk 2:3 says "...yet for the appointed time it hastens toward the goal and it will not fail. Though it tarries, wait for it; for it will certainly come, it will not delay" (Habakkuk 2:3, NASB).

Scriptures of Affirmation
My God is on time

- Psalm 90:4: For a thousand years in Your sight are like yesterday when it passes by, or as a watch in the night (NASB).

- Psalm 105:8: He remembers his covenant forever, the promise he made, for a thousand generations (NIV).

- 2 Peter 3:8: But do not let this one fact escape your notice, beloved, that with the Lord one day is like a thousand years, and a thousand years like one day (NASB).

- Habakkuk 2:3: For the vision is yet for the appointed time it hastens toward the goal and it will not fail. Though it tarries, wait for it; for it will certainly come, it will not delay (NASB).

- Jeremiah 1:12: The Lord said to me, 'You have seen correctly, for I am watching to see that my word is fulfilled (NIV).

- Ecclesiastes 3:1: There is an appointed time for everything. And there is a time for every event under heaven (NASB).

- Hebrews 13:8: Jesus Christ is the same yesterday and today and forever (NIV).

- Ecclesiastes 3:11: He has made everything beautiful in its time. Also, He has put eternity in their hearts, except that no one can find out the work that God does from beginning to end (NKJV).

- Isaiah 41:4: Who has performed and done it, calling the generations from the beginning? I, the Lord, am the first; And with the last I am He (NKJV).

- Galatians 4:4-5: But when the fullness of the time had come, God sent forth His Son, born of a woman, born under the law, to redeem those who were under the law, that we might receive the adoption as sons (NKJV).

- Ezekiel 12:25: But I the Lord will speak what I will, and it shall be fulfilled without delay. For in your days, you rebellious people, I will fulfil whatever I say, declares the Sovereign Lord (NIV).

- Romans 8:28-30: And we know that all things work together for good to those who love God, to those who are the called according to His purpose. For whom He foreknew, He also predestined to be conformed to the image of His Son, that He might be the firstborn among many brethren. Moreover, whom He predestined, these He also called; whom He called, these He also justified; and whom He justified, these He also glorified (NKJV).

- Lamentations 3:25-26: The Lord is my portion," says my soul, Therefore I hope in Him! "The Lord is good to those who wait for

Him, To the soul who seeks Him. It is good that one should hope and wait quietly for the salvation of the Lord (NKJV).

- Psalm 27:14: Wait on the Lord Be of good courage, and He shall strengthen your heart; Wait, I say, on the Lord! (NKJV).

- Genesis 18:14: Is anything too hard for the Lord? At the appointed time I will return to you, according to the time of life, and Sarah shall have a son (NKJV).

- Isaiah 55:11-12: As the rain and the snow come down from heaven and do not return to it without watering the earth and making it bud and flourish so that it yields seed for the sower and bread for the eater so is my word that goes out from my mouth: it will not return to me empty but will accomplish what I desire and achieve the purpose for which I sent it (NIV).

- Revelation 3:14: And to the angel of the church of the Laodiceans write, these things says the Amen, the Faithful and True Witness, the Beginning of the creation of God (NKJV).

Prayer

Father, in Jesus Name, I thank you, for Your faithfulness. I thank You, for everything that you have planned for me. I trust in your perfect timing for everything that pertains to my life. Thank you, Lord, that a time is coming that You will fulfill every promise You have made for me. Lord, I bless you for hearing my prayers and bringing all your promises concerning me to pass. I declare that everything that pertains to me will happen at the right time and without delay. In the Name of Jesus Christ, I cast out and remove any hinderance and interference to everything you have for me. I ask that you release your angels to intervene for me just as you did for

Daniel (see [29]Daniel 10:10-12). Lord, let your angels bring me the answers and instructions. I also thank you for what you have started doing, and for your assignments in my life. I thank you, that you have already seen the successful end. I pray now for your continual guidance, strength, and wisdom, in each step, as I journey. Thank you, Lord, for seeing this assignment through with me to completion. In Jesus Name I pray, Amen.

---

[29] Scripture quotations identified throughout this book in KJV (King James Version), NKJV (New King James Versions), NLT (New Living Translation Version), AMPC(Amplified Version Classic Edition),AMP, (Amplified Bible), ESV(English Standard Version), NIV(New International Version), and NASB (New American Standard Bible) and others indicated are from www.biblegateway.com

THE GOD WHO REMEMBERS

Genesis 30:22-24 -Then God remembered Rachel, and God listened to her and opened her womb and she conceived and bore a son, and said, "God has taken away my reproach. So, she called his name Joseph, and said, "The Lord shall add to me another son" (NKJV).

Scripture Application

Have you ever thought that God had forgotten you? Well I have! There were times when I felt that God had forgotten my prayer requests. Also, I have felt forgotten and alone in times of adversity. Such thoughts were often repeated whenever I saw others get results faster than I did. At times, I even compared myself to them! Isn't it amazing when we look at people, who are not in close relationship with God, and they get their prayers answered, while we are still waiting? We are not called to judge or compare ourselves with others. God shows no partiality, He rains on the unjust and the just (see Mathew 5:45). Psalm 49:16-17 says, *"Do not be afraid when one becomes rich, when the glory of his house is increased; for when he dies, he shall carry nothing away his glory shall not descend after him"* (NKJV). This Scripture simply means, do not worry, envy, or compare where you are with someone who you feel is better than you, because whatever they may have will be left behind when they die. However, have confidence in God, that If He shows no partiality, your turn will come soon!

In Scripture, (Genesis 30:22-24; NKJV), God remembered Rachel, after several years of bareness. Rachel's sister, Leah, had already had six sons and one daughter, before Rachel had had a child. The entire chapter has the account of Rachel's cries and her frustration, and the options she chose to have children. You, too, may have a dire issue, an issue that has been longstanding, or even an issue that has been used by others to ridicule, flatter or laugh at you. Despite the frustration, and temptation, to seek alternative means for meeting the needs, trust God. God still remembers. Like with Rachel, God is attentive to our cries; *"He grants the righteous their desires"* (see Psalm 37:3-4; NKJV). God will remember you as well.

If you feel you are too far gone, that there is no hope for your situation, do not give up. We serve a God who knows His own and would leave everything for just one person. God remembers and goes after that one lost sheep. This is the power of His love. *"What do you think? If a man has a hundred sheep, and one of them goes astray, does he not leave the ninety-nine and go to the mountains to seek the one that is straying? And if he should find it, assuredly, I say to you, he rejoices more over that sheep than over the ninety-nine that did not go astray. Even so it is not the will of your Father who is in heaven that one of these little ones should perish"* (Matthew 18:12-14; NKJV).

God also remembers your good deeds and rewards them accordingly. I love the prayers Nehemiah made to God; he often prayed, *"God remember my good deeds,"* (Nehemiah 13:14; NKJV); *"Remember me, O my God, concerning this, and do not wipe out my good deeds that I have done for the house of my God, and for its services"* (NKJV); and Nehemiah 13:31; *"Remember me, O my God, for good!"* (NKJV).

Continue to serve God sincerely, knowing that a much greater reward awaits. God may reward you here on earth, but you may, or may not physically see your rewards, but you never know the seeds you have sown, or the impact you made. 1Corinthians 15: 57 says *"Therefore, my beloved brethren, be steadfast, immovable, always abounding in the work of the Lord, knowing that your labor is not in vain in the Lord"* (NKJV).

The following Scriptures are accounts of people God remembered. The Bible teaches that these accounts were written for us to know that God can still do the same for us. Approach God persistently in prayer knowing that He will not forget your prayers. God remembers!

Scriptures of Affirmation:
My God is a promise -keeper

- Genesis 8:1: But God remembered Noah and all the beasts and all the livestock that were with him in the ark. And God made a wind blow over the earth, and the waters subsided (ESV).

- 1 Samuel 1:67: *And her rival used to provoke her grievously to irritate her, because the Lord had closed her womb. So, it went on year by year. As often as she went up to the house of the Lord, she used to provoke her. Therefore, Hannah wept and would not eat (ESV).* **1 Samuel 1: 19-20-** They rose early in the morning and worshiped before the Lord; then they went back to their house at Ramah. And Elkanah knew Hannah his wife, **and the Lord remembered her**. And in due time Hannah conceived and bore a son, and she called his name Samuel, for she said, "I have asked for him from the Lord" (ESV).

- Isaiah 49:15-16: But Zion has said, "Yahweh has forsaken me. My Lord has forgotten me—I'm all alone." Yahweh responds, "But how could a loving mother forget her nursing child and not deeply love the one she bore? Even if a there is a mother who forgets her child, I could never, no never, forget you. Can't you see? I have carved your name on the palms of my hands! Your walls are always my concern" (TPT).

- Exodus 2:24-25: So God heard their groaning, and God remembered His covenant with Abraham, with Isaac, and with Jacob. And God looked upon the children of Israel, and God acknowledged them (NKJV).

- Psalm 98:2-3: Everyone knows how God has saved us for he has displayed his justice throughout history. He never forgets to show us his love and faithfulness. How kind he has been to Israel! All the nations know how he stands behind his people and how he saves his own (TPT).

- Ezekiel 16:60: Nevertheless, I will remember My covenant with you in the days of your youth, and I will establish an everlasting covenant with you (NKJV).

- Hebrews 6:10-12: For God is not unjust to forget your work and labor of love which you have shown toward His name, in that you have ministered to the saints, and do minister. And we desire that each one of you show the same diligence to the full assurance of hope until the end, that you do not become sluggish, but imitate those who through faith and patience inherit the promises (NKJV).

- Jeremiah 32:19: Great are You (Lord) in counsel and mighty in deeds, whose eyes are open to all the ways of the sons of men, to reward or repay each one according to his ways and according to the fruit of his doings (AMPC).

- Psalm 37:3-6: Trust in the Lord and do good; dwell in the land and enjoy safe pasture. Take delight in the Lord, and he will give you the desires of your heart. Commit your way to the Lord; trust in him and he will do this: He will make your righteous reward shine like the dawn, your vindication like the noonday sun ([30]NIV).

---

[30] Scripture quotations identified throughout this book in KJV (King James Version), NKJV (New King James Versions), NLT (New Living Translation Version), AMPC(Amplified Version Classic Edition),AMP, (Amplified Bible), ESV(English Standard Version), NIV(New International Version), and NASB (New American Standard Bible) and others indicated are from www.biblegateway.com

Prayer

Father, in the Name of Jesus, I thank you, for your faithfulness. I praise you Lord for being the God who remembers. Thank you, for the great rewards you have for me; I look forward to them with joy.

Lord, I forgive everyone (name the person) who has mocked, laughed, or ridiculed me, because of this missing issue in my life. I release them and let them go. I renounce any bitterness, resentment, or harsh feelings towards them. I command any trauma associated with their comments and actions, out of my DNA, blood system, heart, mind, and body. I appropriate the Blood of Jesus Christ to cleanse me inside and out, and to remove all toxins related to such trauma. I am renewed afresh. Lord, fill me with Your Spirit, and with your love for these people or person (name the person) in Jesus Name. Father God, I renounce and cast out anything that has contributed to delays in my life. I command them out in Jesus Name. I now activate acceleration and momentum in my life, henceforth, in Jesus Name!

Now Lord, I submit this issue to you (be specific and name the need). Lord, you know my desires, and you are exceedingly capable of meeting them. Out of your abundant mercy, love and faithfulness grant this desire, remember my need, oh Lord. I give you praise, glory and honor that you have heard my prayer and granted my desires. Lord, you have remembered me. I now thank you in advance for the perfect timing of your answer. You make all things beautiful in Your time. You have remembered me. Thank you, Lord. In Jesus Name I pray. Amen.

THE GOD WHO SEES

Genesis 16:13-Then she called the name of the Lord who spoke to her, **You-Are-the-God Who-Sees**; for she said, "Have I also here seen Him who sees me? (NKJV)

Scripture Application

Some adversities in life can make us think that no one cares. Such moments of desperation can result in our making blanket statements such as "no one cares", or "God does not care." We often find ourselves lonely; having no one to turn to. Or these could be moments where we face unfairness and injustice, as well as rejection and abandonment. Haggar faced such conditions when Sarah, her mistress, kicked her out of her home.

Haggar's story is narrated in Genesis chapter 16. In summary, Sarah asked Abraham to send Haggar and her son away, because Haggar despised Sarah for not having children. Haggar then ended up in a desert with little food left to feed her son. So, she opted to distance herself from her son, so as not to watch him die. God, however, heard the cry of Haggar's son and intervened. First, by showing her where to get water to drink, and secondly, with instructions of what to do next. Haggar's response was "I have seen the One who sees me."

God sees each desperate moment. Whether injustice was done, or whether the adversity is of our own making. God sees it all and is still merciful to respond when we call on Him. I encourage you to still call on God, especially at your most vulnerable time, when you feel alone, or when all hope for breakthrough is gone - this could be your desert moment, still call on the God who sees.

Are there situations that you have no solutions for? Maybe it is a child who has gone astray, or maybe it is something you have lost and cannot locate, or it could be something buried deep within you that needs to be unearthed in order to experience freedom. Call on the God who sees.

Calling on the God who sees is also crucial when have to engage with people. Ask the Lord to expose the intents and motives of the people you want to partner with in business or partner with for a common cause. God sees and knows the intents of each person's heart. The God who sees will expose them to you.

When you have questions about certain things God will show you answers. God is able to show us what is to come, the secrets, the treasures, the unseen and unheard. God sees all. He is ready to engage with us in deep conversations. When we ask Him, God will also open our spiritual eyes to see, through dreams, visions, or encounters with Him. Call on the God who sees.

Finally, at times, we are all affected with things that we cannot see with our eyes, and we need spiritual eyes, but we also need God to unearth and expose those areas so we can be healed and restored to fellowship with Him. In such situations we cry, *"God, search my heart and remove that which is hidden, remove all that is standing in the way of breakthrough, or communion with you."* The Lord sees everything. So, search my heart oh Lord (see Psalm 139: 23-24; ESV).

Scriptures of Affirmation:
The Lord eyes are on me

- Proverbs 15:3: The eyes of the Lord are in every place, keeping watch on the evil and the good (ESV).

- Psalms 33:13-15: The Lord looks down from heaven; He sees all the children of man; from where He sits enthroned, he looks out on all the inhabitants of the earth, He who fashions the hearts of them all and observes all their deeds (ESV).

- Jeremiah 23:23-24: Am I a God at hand, declares the Lord, and not a God far away? Can a man hide himself in secret places so that I cannot see him? declares the Lord. Do I not fill heaven and earth? declares the Lord (ESV).

- Jeremiah 17:10: I, the Lord, search the heart, I test the mind even to give every man according to his ways according to the fruit of his doings (NKJV).

- Proverbs 21:2: Every way of a man is right in his own eyes, but the Lord weighs the hearts (NKJV).

- Job 34: 21-22: For God's eyes are upon the ways of a man, and He sees all his steps. There is no darkness nor thick gloom where the evildoers may hide themselves (AMPC).

- 1 Samuel 16:7: But the Lord said to Samuel, "Do not look on his appearance or on the height of his stature, because I have rejected him. For the Lord sees not as man sees man looks on the outward appearance, but the Lord looks on the heart (ESV).

- Hebrews 4:13: And no creature is hidden from his sight, but all are naked and exposed to the eyes of him to whom we must give account (ESV).

- Jeremiah 16:17: For My eyes are on all their ways; they are not hidden from My face, neither is their iniquity concealed from My eyes (AMPC).

- Psalm 139:23-24: Search me thoroughly O God and know my heart! Try me and know my thoughts and see if there is any wicked or hurtful way in me and lead me in the way everlasting ([31]NKJV).

Prayer

Father, in the Name of Jesus, I thank you, for watching over me. I am grateful that I am the apple of your eye. Lord, you see and know every detail of my life. I pray that you show me what I need to know about my life's destiny, and what I need to do to accomplish it. I pray also that you search my heart, and life, and show me what is standing in the way of communion with you. Lord, I forgive everyone who has committed injustice towards me, I release them, and ask you to judge them instead. I pray Lord, that you will expose them to your truth about the matter. Lord, I pray now that you show me the secrets and treasures that you have for me. Give me wisdom, knowledge and understanding of them. I thank you Lord. In Jesus Name, Amen.

---

[31] Scripture quotations identified throughout this book in KJV (King James Version), NKJV (New King James Versions), NLT (New Living Translation Version), AMPC(Amplified Version Classic Edition),AMP, (Amplified Bible), ESV(English Standard Version), NIV(New International Version), and NASB (New American Standard Bible) and others indicated are from www.biblegateway.com

ALL CONSUMING FIRE

Deuteronomy 9:3 -Therefore understand today that the Lord your God is He who goes over before you as a consuming fire. He will destroy them and bring them down before you; so, you shall drive them out and destroy them quickly, as the Lord has said to you (NKJV).

Scripture Application

There are different functions of the Fire of God in our lives including: purification, refining, baptism, activation, impartation, power, illumination, and God's glory. The Consuming Fire aspect of God involves defense, protection and destruction of sin and wickedness.

There are aspects of sanctification that involve the Consuming Fire of God. In Hebrews we are told that our God is a consuming fire, and that He will shake things so that what remains cannot be shaken. As believers we should expect God to "shake the house and remove whatever does not need to be there." This process is often painful, but should be embraced, with the understanding that God is holy and His sanctification by fire is a product of walking with Him in holiness. Hebrews 12:27-29 says *"The words "once more" indicate the removing of what can be shaken—that is, created things—so* that what cannot be shaken may remain. Therefore, since we are receiving a kingdom that cannot be shaken, let us be thankful, and so worship God acceptably with reverence and awe for our 'God is a consuming fire'" (NIV).

God deals with issues of idolatry and sin with His Consuming Fire. God desires that all aspects of our lives are dedicated to Him, and that our lives do not involve idolatry or witchcraft. In this age we can be caught up in forms of idolatry. This is often limited to the worship of other gods but can also include material things or things that keep us so preoccupied that we neglect God, and, therefore, do not serve Him with total commitment. Scripture says in Deuteronomy 4:23-24: *"Take care, lest you forget the covenant of the Lord your God, which he made with you, and make a carved image, the form of anything that the Lord your God has forbidden you. For the Lord, your God is a consuming fire, a jealous God "*(ESV).

The Consuming Fire, as God's defense, functions in delivering us from works and schemes of the devil. God will use His Consuming Fire to fight entities and everything that is opposed to His people and to His purposes. Scripture tells us in Deuteronomy 9:3 -*Know therefore today that he who goes over before you as a consuming fire is the Lord your God. He will destroy them and subdue them before you. So, you shall drive them out and make them perish quickly, as the Lord has promised you"* (ESV).

God's fire as a hedge of protection. At times we pray to God, "let your fire go before us." We know the Israelites were led by a Fire at night and by a Cloud in the day. The Fire of the Lord shall go before us and His glory is behind us. Exodus 13: 21-22 says *"And the Lord went before them by day in a pillar of cloud to lead them along the way, and by night in a pillar of fire to give them light, that they might travel by day and by night. The pillar of cloud by day and the pillar of fire by night did not depart from before the people"* (ESV).

Scriptures of Affirmation
The Lord protects me

- Exodus 18:19: Now Mount Sinai was wrapped in smoke because the Lord had descended on it in fire. The smoke of it went up like the smoke of a kiln, and the whole mountain trembled greatly (ESV).

- Isaiah 30:27-30: Behold, the name of the Lord comes from afar, burning with his anger, and in thick rising smoke; his lips are full of fury, and his tongue is like a devouring fire; his breath is like an overflowing stream that reaches up to the neck; to sift the nations with the sieve of destruction, and to place on the jaws of the peoples a bridle that leads astray. You shall have a song as in the night when a holy feast is kept, and gladness of heart, as when one sets out to the sound of the flute to go to the mountain of the Lord, to the Rock of Israel. And the Lord will cause his majestic voice to be heard and the descending blow of his arm to be seen, in furious anger and a flame of devouring fire, with a cloudburst and storm and hailstones (ESV).

- Deuteronomy 9:3: Therefore, understand today that the Lord your God is He who goes over before you as a consuming fire. He will destroy them and bring them down before you; so, you shall drive them out and destroy them quickly, as the Lord has said to you (NKJV).

- Hebrews 12:27-29: The words "once more" indicate the removing of what can be shaken—that is, created things—so that what cannot be shaken may remain. Therefore, since we are receiving a kingdom that cannot be shaken, let us be thankful, and so worship God acceptably with reverence and awe for our "God is a consuming fire (NIV).

- Exodus 13: 21-22: says; and the Lord went before them by day in a pillar of cloud to lead them along the way, and by night in a pillar of fire to give them light, that they might travel by day and by night. The pillar of cloud by day and the pillar of fire by night did not depart from before the people (ESV).

- Deuteronomy 4:23-24: Take care, lest you forget the covenant of the Lord your God, which he made with you, and make a carved image, the form of anything that the Lord your God has forbidden you. For the Lord, your God is a consuming fire, a jealous God (ESV).

- Matthew 10:28: And do not fear those who kill the body but cannot kill the soul. Rather fear him who can destroy both soul and body in hell (ESV).

- Isaiah 33:14: The sinners in Zion are afraid; trembling has seized the godless: "Who among us can dwell with the consuming fire? Who among us can dwell with everlasting burnings? (ESV).

- Jeremiah 17:27: But if you do not listen to me, to keep the Sabbath day holy, and not to bear a burden and enter by the gates of Jerusalem on the Sabbath day, then I will kindle a fire in its gates, and it shall devour the palaces of Jerusalem and shall not be quenched (ESV).

- Zechariah 2:5: And I will be to her a wall of fire all around, declares the Lord, and I will be the glory in her midst ([32]ESV).

---

[32] Scripture quotations identified throughout this book in KJV (King James Version), NKJV (New King James Versions), NLT (New Living Translation Version), AMPC(Amplified Version Classic Edition),AMP, (Amplified Bible), ESV(English Standard Version), NIV(New International Version), and NASB (New American Standard Bible) and others indicated are from www.biblegateway.com

Prayer

Father, in the Name of Jesus, I acknowledge you as The Consuming Fire. Thank you, for your purging and refining. Lord, I submit myself to you to shake off everything that needs to be shaken off internally and externally. Let your fire burn and consume all, that I may be pure before you. Lord, I repent of any areas of iniquity, transgression and of the sin of idolatry, in any form, in my life and bloodline. I repent and ask for your forgiveness. I renounce all forms of idolatry and sorcery. I ask that the blood of Jesus cleanse and purify my bloodline and my DNA. I ask Lord for your consuming fire to burn away completely the roots of idolatry, witchcraft, abominations, and sin of any kind in my life, in the Name of Jesus. Father, I now engage your Consuming Fire for deliverance and protection. Deter the darts of the enemy by your fire. Let your fire be a hedge of protection around me and your glory within me, in Jesus Name I pray. Amen.

THE ANCIENT OF DAYS

CHAPTER 25

Daniel 7:9-10- I watched till thrones were put in place, and the Ancient of Days was seated; His garment was white as snow and the hair of His head was like pure wool. His throne was a fiery flame, its wheels a burning fire; a fiery stream issue and came forth from before Him. A thousand thousands ministered to Him; ten thousand times ten thousand stood before Him. The court was seated, and the books were opened (NKJV).

Scripture Application

I had actually finished writing this book and was finalizing it for publication, when while petitioning God in my prayer time, I heard myself call for the Ancient of Days. I recall saying "Lord, I call on you as the Ancient of Days, to go to the root of this issue and vindicate me." This was my first time using this title and I was surprised by that utterance in my prayer. The issue I was petitioning God for was a generational bloodline issue; a family issue that impacted the maternal side of my family. I wanted God to intervene and bring deliverance and breakthrough. I believe the utterance to call upon God as the Ancient of Days to deal with the situation was given at the unction of the Holy Spirit.

I have come to value this Name when praying about generational issues; we often lack the specifics of what happened in the past. Some experiences are passed down from generation to generation, but without details. In such situations, I have now learned to call upon the Ancient of Days. He saw everything from its inception, all the details of what happened; and He has the power and authority to vindicate me and to vindicate you. The Ancient of Days refers to God being present at the beginning, ageless and timeless. The infinite, unchanging, endless God!

I encourage you to call on the Ancient of Days when you experience things you do not understand; and, also as you deal with generational issues of the past. Ask Him to war for you as roots of negative experiences in your life are exposed. See His judgement and vindication on behalf of the saints in **Daniel 7: 21-22**; *"I kept looking, and that horn was waging war with the saints and overpowering them* **until the Ancient of Days came and judgment was passed in favor of the saints of the Highest One, and the time arrived when the saints took possession of the kingdom"** (NASB). As the Ancient of Days, God is the Beginning and the End, meaning He sees the end from the beginning. He saw everything before we were conceived. A thousand years are like a day to Him, meaning God is able to see the past in real time. Although the vision Daniel saw was related to the end times, we too can anticipate the same vindication for the righteous who are currently on the earth, and that is us!

Scriptures of Affirmation
God of all times

- Psalm 90:1-2: Lord, You have been our dwelling place in all generations. Before the mountains were born Or You gave birth to the earth and the world. Even from everlasting to everlasting, You are God (NASB).

- Daniel 7:13-14: I was watching in the night visions, and behold, One like the Son of Man, coming with the clouds of heaven! He came to the Ancient of Days, and they brought Him near before Him. Then to Him was given dominion and glory and a kingdom, that all peoples, nations, and languages should serve Him. His dominion is an everlasting dominion, which shall not pass away, and His kingdom the one which shall not be destroyed (NKJV).

- Genesis 1:1: In the beginning God created the heavens and the earth. The earth was without form, and void; and darkness [a]was on the face of the deep. And the Spirit of God was hovering over the face of the waters (NKJV).

- Hebrews 13:8: Jesus Christ is the same yesterday and today and forever (NIV).

- Psalm 90:3-4: You turn man back into dust and say, "Return, O children of men. "For a thousand years in Your sight are like yesterday when it passes by, Or as a watch in the night (NASB).

- Isaiah 44:6-8: Thus says the Lord, the King of Israel and his Redeemer, the Lord of hosts: **I am the first and I am the last and there is no God besides Me**. Who is like Me? Let him proclaim and declare it; Yes, let him recount it to Me in order. From the time that I established the ancient nation and let them declare to them the things that are coming and the events that are going to take place. Do not tremble and do not be afraid; Have I not long since announced it to you and declared it? And you are My witnesses. Is there any God besides Me Or is there any other Rock? know of none (NASB).

- Exodus 20:4-6: You shall not make for yourself [c]an idol, or any likeness of what is in heaven above or on the earth beneath or in the water under the earth. You shall not worship them or serve them; for I, the Lord your God, am a jealous God, visiting the iniquity of the fathers on the children, on the third and the fourth generations of those who hate Me, but showing lovingkindness to thousands, to those who love Me and keep My commandments ([33]NASB).

Prayer

Father God, I worship and adore You as the Ancient of Days. From everlasting to everlasting, You are God. You are God of my past, present and future. Lord, I repent of any actions on my part in the past that are negatively affecting my life now in the present. In Your mercy and grace Lord, I ask You to vindicate me. Lord, I repent of all generational bloodline issues, sins, iniquities, covenants, pacts, and agreements. I renounce them all in Jesus Name. Now I pray Lord, that you would exonerate me and loose me from them in Jesus Name. Lord, vindicate me in Your justice, truth and righteousness concerning each stage of my life from the time I was conceived to the last day of my life on earth. Lord, cover me in Your divine protection from all evil that would try to impact my present and future generations. Lord, protect me from anything that would impact my walk with You now and in the future. Thank you, Lord, that with You on my side I am victoriously walking in the fullness of my destiny in Jesus Name. Amen

[33] Scripture quotations identified throughout this book in KJV (King James Version), NKJV (New King James Versions), NLT (New Living Translation Version), AMPC(Amplified Version Classic Edition),AMP, (Amplified Bible), ESV(English Standard Version), NIV(New International Version), and NASB (New American Standard Bible) and others indicated are from www.biblegateway.com

THE GOOD GOD WHOSE MERCY ENDURES FOREVER

Psalm 100.5 For the Lord is good; His mercy is everlasting, and His truth endures to all generations.

Scripture Application

You may already be familiar with the greeting or expression "God is good" which is often responded to with "and goodness is His nature" or "all the time". God 's goodness and are sure to God's nature that they endure forever. I often reflect on my testimony when it comes to God's goodness and mercies. Although I received Jesus at twelve years old, I backslide after relocating to the USA. Most of my young adult life was backslidden until the re-dedicated my life to God in my mid-thirties. I am still in awe of God's mercies, goodness, and love; that He still preserved my life, allowing me to eventually pursue the destiny He had for me.

The entire chapters of Psalm 103 and Psalm 107 were instrumental in my restoration. For instance, Psalm 103 *starts with Bless the Lord, O my soul; and all that is within me, bless His holy name! Bless the Lord, O my soul, and forget not all His benefits: who forgives all your iniquities, Who heals all your diseases, who redeems your life from destruction, who crowns you with lovingkindness and tender mercies, who satisfies your mouth with good things, so that your youth is renewed like the eagle's. (Psalm 103:1-5, NKJV).* The rest of this Psalm is about God's goodness in forgiving our sins, in not dealing with us according to our transgressions, in caring for us as a loving father would do and in providing for us. These attributes serve as constant reminder that God deals with us very differently compared to how fellow humans would deal with us- in these we see how His goodness and mercies are immeasurable. These attributes also show the sincerity of God's heart towards His children when they repent. Above all, these attributes trump fear, guilty, shame and condemnation for anyone who thinks they have gone too far from God, and anyone who feels God will respond to them with punishment! The goodness of God is captured in this Psalm. Although I have since pursued a righteous life, I still use these scriptures for repentance and also to break strongholds, lies and false believes that may present as "God may be punishing me for my past". Certainly, we must face the consequences of our poor chooses; but God does not deal with us according to our sins. See Psalm 103: 6-10; (NKJV).

Psalm 107 is about God's great works and deliverance; I have several testimonies of God's deliverance from the process of being born through my adulthood. Psalm 107 is a prayer of thanksgiving in response to God's deliverance. *This Psalm too starts with Oh, give thanks to the Lord, for He is good for His mercy endures forever. Let the redeemed of the Lord say so, Whom He has redeemed from the hand of the enemy* (Psalm 107:1-2; NKJV). In the Old Testament, God's goodness and mercies were reflected on actual sang bring the nation victory. Jehoshaphat's example is a great one. See 2 Chronicles 20: 21-22- *and when he had consulted with the people, he appointed those who should sing to the Lord, and who should praise the beauty of holiness, as they went out before the army and were saying:* **"Praise the Lord, For His mercy endures forever.** *"Now when they began to sing and to praise, the Lord set ambushes against the people of Ammon, Moab, and Mount Seir, who had come against Judah; and they were defeated. (NKJV)*

Regardless of where you have been or what you have done, remember that God is good! We may not see the goodness in what we may be experiencing, but God does not send bad things to us, the devil does; some negative experiences though are because of our lack of knowledge (ignorance) and poor chooses. Also know that God is merciful, there is nothing that He cannot forgive and restore if we repent and seek Him with a sincere heart. Repentance removes shame and guilt; this allows us to enjoy the freedom we have been afforded by Christ Jesus.

Scriptures of Affirmation
My God is merciful towards me

- Lamentations 3: 22- 26-Through the Lord's mercies we are not consumed, because His compassions fail not. They are new every morning; great is Your faithfulness. The Lord is my portion," says my soul, therefore I hope in Him!" The Lord is good to those who wait for Him, to the soul who seeks Him. It is good that one should hope and wait quietly for the salvation of the Lord. (NKJV)

- Exodus 33:19 -presence. I will have mercy on whom I will have mercy, and I will have compassion on whom I will have compassion

- Exodus 34: 5-7 -Then the Lord came down in the cloud and stood there with Him and proclaimed His name, the Lord. And He passed in front of Moses, proclaiming, "The Lord, the Lord, the compassionate and gracious God, slow to anger, abounding in love and faithfulness, maintaining love to thousands, and forgiving wickedness, rebellion and sin. Yet He does not leave the guilty unpunished; he punishes the children and their children for the sin of the parents to the third and fourth generation." (NIV)

- Psalm 31:19-20- Oh, how abundant is Your goodness, which You have stored up for those who fear you and worked for those who take refuge in You, in the sight of the children of mankind! In the cover of your presence you hide them from the plots of men; you store them in your shelter from the strife of tongues. (ESV)

- And we know that all things work together for good to those who love God, to those who are the called according to His purpose.

- Psalm 27:13-14 I believe that I shall look upon the goodness of the Lord in the land of the living! Wait for the Lord; be strong, and let your heart take courage; wait for the Lord! (ESV)

- Psalm 119:68- You are good, and what you do is good; teach me your decrees. (NIV)

- Psalm 23:6 Surely goodness and mercy shall follow me all the days of my life and I shall dwell in the house of the Lord forever [34](ESV)

Prayer

Father in Jesus name I acknowledge You as a good God. Thank you for your goodness and mercies that are you provide me daily. I thank you for your mercies that are new every day. I bless your name for the deliverance, protection, provision and even chastening that you have given me out of your tender loving kindness and mercies for me. Thank you, Lord, for being patient with me abd always drawing me back to you. Thank you for fighting my battles and vindicating me. In all things, I worship and adore you- I declare that God you are good, and your mercies endure forever. Amen

---

[34] Scripture quotations identified throughout this book in KJV (King James Version), NKJV (New King James Versions), NLT (New Living Translation Version), AMPC(Amplified Version Classic Edition),AMP, (Amplified Bible), ESV(English Standard Version), NIV(New International Version), and NASB (New American Standard Bible) and others indicated are from www.biblegateway.com

THE LORD RESTORES

Joel 2: 25-27- So I will restore to you the years that the swarming locust has eaten. The crawling locust, the consuming locust, and the chewing locust. My great army which I sent among you. You shall eat in plenty and be satisfied and praise the name of the Lord your God who has dealt wondrously with you and My people shall never be put to shame. Then you shall know that I am in the midst of Israel: I am the Lord your God and there is no other. My people shall never be put to shame (NKJV).

Scripture Application

What better way to conclude this book than with the assurance that God restores? If by any chance you feel you lost time, resources, or relationships, for one reason or another, know that God will restore. There are things we have to discard and there are relationships we need to end out of obedience to God. And then there are the things that the enemy stole or destroyed. And we like Job should be assured that God is faithful to restore all that was lost.

We are currently living in a season of uncertainty. There is a major medical crisis occurring throughout the world. Global economies have been affected, businesses have incurred major losses, there are job furloughs and most people are unemployed. Nevertheless, God remains faithful. He is not moved by what is happening. He still promises restoration for the righteous, both spiritually and materially. After his adversity, God restored Job with a double portion of possessions as well as a double portion of children. "And *the Lord restored Job's losses when he prayed for his friends. Indeed, the Lord gave Job twice as much as he had before. After this Job lived one hundred and forty years and saw his children and grandchildren for four generations*" (Job 42:10; 16; NKJV). Job's adversity mirrors what is happening in the world today, where all sectors of our livelihood are affected, but as God came through for Job, He will also come through for us.

As you petition God for your needs using the attributes that are given in this book, be confident that your prayers have not been in vain. God honors and responds to the prayers of the righteous. Make known to God everything that you have lost. Ask Him to restore as He promises. Below are Scriptures that you can declare and use in your prayers. Expect your restoration!

Scriptures of Affirmation
I will recover better things and much more

- Isaiah 61:7: Instead of your shame there shall be a double portion; instead of dishonor they shall rejoice in their lot; therefore in their land they shall possess a double portion; they shall have everlasting joy (ESV).

- Psalm 71:19-21: Also, Your righteousness, O God, is very high, You who have done great things. O God, who is like You? You, who have shown me great and severe troubles, shall revive me again, and bring me up again from the depths of the earth. You shall increase my greatness, and comfort me on every side (NKJV).

- Jeremiah 30:17: For I will restore health to you, and your wounds I will heal, declares the LORD, because they have called you an outcast: 'It is Zion, for whom no one cares! (ESV).

- Amos 9:14: I will restore the fortunes of my people Israel, and they shall rebuild the ruined cities and inhabit them; they shall plant vineyards and drink their wine, and they shall make gardens and eat their fruit (ESV).

- Deuteronomy 30:1-3: And when all these things come upon you, the blessing and the curse, which I have set before you, and you call them to mind among all the nations where the Lord your God has driven you, and return to the Lord your God, you and your children, and obey his voice in all that I command you today, with all your heart and with all your soul, then the Lord your God will restore your fortunes and have mercy on you, and he will gather you again from all the peoples where the Lord your God has scattered you (ESV).

- Proverbs 6:30-31: People do not despise a thief if he steals to satisfy his appetite when he is hungry, but if he is caught, he will pay sevenfold; he will give all the goods of his house (ESV). This Scripture has been applied in this section outlining Satan as the thief.

- Psalm 30:5: For His anger is but for a moment, His favor is for life; weeping may endure for a night, but joy comes in the morning ([35]NKJV).

---

[35] Scripture quotations identified throughout this book in KJV (King James Version), NKJV (New King James Versions), NLT (New Living Translation Version), AMPC(Amplified Version Classic Edition),AMP, (Amplified Bible), ESV(English Standard Version), NIV(New International Version), and NASB (New American Standard Bible) and others indicated are from www.biblegateway.com

Prayer

Father, in the Name of Jesus, I thank you for your promises that are sure. I bless you for being a relatable God, who understands and sees what I have gone through. Lord, I let go of the regrets and the tears of my losses. I ask that you heal me from the pain of the losses. I pray now that you restore my time, resources, and everything that I lost. Thank you, Lord, in advance, because I know you will restore exceedingly more than I have asked. In Jesus Name. Amen

THE OMINISCIENT, OMNIPRESENT, OMNIPOTENT GOD

CHAPTER 28

These three aspects of God sum-up God's nature. All the descriptions of God that have been outlined in previous chapters of this book can be summarized in these. God is the All in All God!

His Omniscience means that God is all knowing. He created all and has knowledge of everything. In a world of immerging technologies and discoveries; God knows what will be discovered, what is being developed, and the current and future impact of those inventions. There is nothing that catches God by surprise! With this we can be assured that as a we abide in Jesus; we will continually be informed of what is coming and what is new. Jeremiah 33: 3 says *"Call to me and I will answer you and will tell you great and hidden things that you have not known"* (ESV). This means there are great and hidden things that God knows about our destiny that we do not know yet; still God is gracious and want us to know these things. Should you have questions, concerns, need direction or information; seek the All-Knowing God!

Omnipresent means that God is always there. This book is being written in the middle of a global crisis that was caused by a lethal virus.

In such times, people may ask where God was or why God allowed this crisis. The truth is that God is present and with us, even now, during the global crisis. He is present with those who are suffering, and with those who have lost loved ones. God is present in times of need and in times of abundance. We, the righteous, know that God is with us amidst crises; and we are preserved and protected by Him. God still delivers and ensures that we are provided for. *"Be strong and of good courage, do not fear nor be afraid of them; for the Lord your God, He is the One who goes with you. He will not leave you nor forsake you"* (see Deuteronomy 31:6, NKJV). Keep your life free from love of money, and be content with what you have, for he has said, *"I will never leave you nor forsake you"* (Hebrews 13:5, ESV). But now, this is what the Lord says *"He who created you, Jacob, He who formed you, Israel. Do not fear, for I have redeemed you; I have summoned you by name; you are mine. When you pass through the waters, I will be with you; and when you pass through the rivers, they will not sweep over you. When you walk through the fire, you will not be burned; the flames will not set you ablaze, for I am the Lord your God"* ([36]Isaiah 43: 1-3, NIV).

Our God, the Omnipotent God! Omnipotent means all powerful! A look at creation itself shows us how powerful God is. I like watching travel and adventure documentaries. Once, I watched a documentary on coral reefs that are under oceans. The documentary showed different species of coral reefs, clothed in different glowing colors. These reefs feed on microorganisms. The fact that God created the microorganisms blew my mind! This is the same God who created the heavens, the mountains, the seasons, the glaciers, the waterfalls. Our God is incomparable. He is mighty in power; He stands alone as God.

---

[36] Scripture quotations identified throughout this book in KJV (King James Version), NKJV (New King James Versions), NLT (New Living Translation Version), AMPC(Amplified Version Classic Edition),AMP, (Amplified Bible), ESV(English Standard Version), NIV(New International Version), and NASB (New American Standard Bible) and others indicated are from www.biblegateway.com

There are many descriptions of God's power, but whenever I read the book of Job, I bow in awe. Job 38 also describes God's awesome power. The depths of God's sovereignty and 's abilities are detailed in these chapters. God's influence is seen in every aspect of creation, from humans, to birds, to sea creatures and to animals. After reading these chapters you can attest of God's majesty. Take time to read in your devotion today.

Let us close this chapter in worship. His omnipotence means nothing is impossible with God. Lord, we bow in worship, we acknowledge your omnipotence, Your majesty, Your power, Your omnipresence, Your wisdom, Your knowledge! Scripture tells us in Jeremiah 32:18-19(NKJV): *"Great and mighty God, whose name is the Lord Almighty, great are your purposes and mighty are your deeds. Your eyes are open to the ways of all mankind; you reward each person according to their conduct and as their deeds deserve."* And Jeremiah continues 32:26-27: *"Then the word of the Lord came to Jeremiah I am the Lord, the God of all mankind. Is anything too hard for me (NKJV)?"* Remember who our God is; One who is there for every situation. You are covered in every area of your life. You have God our Father, who loves you - the Holy God, the I AM, the Almighty God, Yahweh, Adonai. God your provider, peace, defense, banner, deliverer, shepherd, sanctifier; the Lord your righteousness. He is the Lord of justice, righteousness, and truth. The Lord who is there. The Lord who has the keys to open and shut. The Alpha and Omega; God who remembers and God who sees. He is the All-Consuming Fire! Wonderful Counselor, The Mighty God, everlasting Father and Lord of Hosts!

"Now to Him who is able to keep you from stumbling, and to present you faultless before the presence of His glory with exceeding joy, To God our Savior, Who alone is wise, be glory and majesty, dominion, and power, both now and forever. Amen." (Jude 1:25; NJKV).

Let us join the hosts of heaven and the angels in worship-*"And every creature which is in heaven and on the earth and under the earth and such as are in the sea, and all that are in them, I heard saying: blessing and honor and glory and power be to Him who sits on the throne and to the Lamb, forever and ever!* (³⁷Revelation 5:13, NJKV).

Prayer

Father God I will believe your report. No matter what reports are being released out there; Lord I believe Your report. That You are still the faithful God, redeeming God, saving God, delivering God, the just Judge, the unchanging God, the Lord our banner, our Friend in time of need, our Protector and Shield, our defender and true Shepherd. The one who never fails! The God who changes not! Our restorer! Our Provider! Our healer! Lord I believe Your report! I believe Your Word that will never pass away. You are the bread of life, You are life! I believe in You Lord, Almighty God, God of miracles! God of wonders; Powerful God. I believe in You

---

³⁷ Scripture quotations identified throughout this book in KJV (King James Version), NKJV (New King James Versions), NLT (New Living Translation Version), AMPC(Amplified Version Classic Edition),AMP, (Amplified Bible), ESV(English Standard Version), NIV(New International Version), and NASB (New American Standard Bible) and others indicated are from www.biblegateway.com

NAMES AND ATTRIBUTES OF JESUS CHRIST

Our Lord Jesus Christ has many titles and roles that can also be applied in prayer. According to I Timothy 2:5 (ESV), Jesus is our only mediator. He is also our intercessor as He is seated on His throne next to the Father. I believe that when I am praying in tongues – the language of the Spirit - I am aligning myself with the prayers Jesus is making. For this reason, I do not see my devotion time as just myself praying; but I believe that God the Father, God the Son-Jesus Christ, the Holy Spirit and, of course; lots of Angels, are joining with me in prayer. So, in our prayer time or during worship we are never alone.

Names are directly linked to the destiny and the role of a person. I like to reflect on and use the titles of Jesus Christ; applying them respectively to the issue I am praying about. I have also incorporated submitting all areas of my live to the Lordship of Jesus Christ and in prayer. Listed below area titles that can be used; I have condensed this list, but I am sure there are more-feel free to apply them:

♥ *King of kings-and Lord of lords-* These will make war with the Lamb, and the Lamb will overcome them, for He is Lord of lords and King of kings; and those who are with Him are called, chosen, and faithful. And He has on His robe and on His thigh a name written: KING OF KINGS AND LORD OF LORDS (Revelation 17:14, Revelation 19:16, NKJV).

♥ *God with us-Immanuel-* Therefore the Lord Himself will give you a sign: Behold, the virgin shall conceive and bear a Son, and shall call His name Immanuel (Isaiah 7:14, NKJV)

♥ *Advocate-* My little children, these things I write to you, so that you may not sin. And if anyone sins, we have an Advocate with the Father, Jesus Christ the righteous (1 John 2:1, NKJV).

♥ *I Am-* Jesus said to them, "Most assuredly, I say to you, before Abraham was, I AM (John 8:58, NKJV).

♥ *Creator-* He is the image of the invisible God, the firstborn over all creation. For by Him all things were created that are in heaven and that are on earth, visible and invisible, whether thrones or dominions or [e]principalities or powers. All things were created through Him and for Him and He is before all things, and in Him all things consist (Colossians 1:16-17, ESV).

♥ *Head of the Church-* And He is the head of the body, the church, who is the beginning, the firstborn from the dead, that in all things He may have the preeminence (Colossians 1:16-17, Ephesians 4:12, ESV).

♥ *Great High Priest-* Therefore, since we have a great high priest who has ascended into heaven, Jesus the Son of God, let us hold firmly to the faith we profess (Hebrews 4:14, NIV).

♥ *Author and Perfecter of our faith-* looking to Jesus, the founder and perfecter of our faith, who for the joy that was set before him endured the cross, despising the shame, and is seated at the right hand of the throne of God (Hebrews 12:2, ESV).

- ♥ *Bread of Life-* Then Jesus declared, "I am the bread of life. Whoever comes to me will never go hungry, and whoever believes in me will never be thirsty (John 6:35, NIV).

- ♥ *The Resurrection and the Life-* Jesus said to her, "I am the resurrection and the life. The one who believes in me will live, even though they die (John11:25, NIV).

- ♥ *Risen Lord-* For what I received I passed on to you as of first importance[a]: that Christ died for our sins according to the Scriptures, 4 that he was buried, that he was raised on the third day according to the Scriptures (1 Corinthians 15:3-4, NIV).

- ♥ *Chief Cornerstone-*The stone the builders rejected has become the cornerstone; the Lord has done this, and it is marvelous in our eyes. The Lord has done it this very day; let us rejoice today and be glad. (Psalm 118-22-24, Ephesians 2:20, NIV).

- ♥ *Deliverer-* and to wait for His Son from heaven, whom He raised from the dead, even Jesus who delivers us from the wrath to come (1 Thessalonians 1:10, NKJV).

- ♥ *Friend-* No longer do I call you servants, for the servant does not know what his master is doing; but I have called you friends, for all that I have heard from my Father I have made known to you (John 15:15, ESV).

- ♥ *Faithful and True-* Now I saw heaven opened, and behold, a white horse. And He who sat on him was called Faithful and True, and in righteousness He judges and makes war (Revelation 19:11, NKJV).

- ♥ *Good Shepherd-* I am the good shepherd; the good shepherd lays down His life for the sheep (John 10: 11, ESV).

- ♥ *High Priest*-Therefore, since we have a great high priest who has ascended into heaven, Jesus the Son of God, let us hold firmly to the faith we profess (Hebrews 4:14, NIV).

- ♥ *Intercessor-* Also there were many priests because they were prevented by death from continuing. But He, because He continues forever, has an unchangeable priesthood. Therefore, He is also able to save to the uttermost those who come to God through Him, since He always lives to make intercession for them (Hebrews 7:23-25, NKJV).

- ♥ *Mediator-* For there is one God, and one mediator also between God and men, the man Christ Jesus (1Timothy 2:5, Hebrews 9:15, Hebrews 12:24, ESV).

- ♥ *Judge-* And He commanded us to preach to the people, and to testify that it is He who was ordained by God to be Judge of the living and the dead (Acts 10:42, NJKV).

- ♥ *Light of the world-* Again Jesus spoke to them, saying, "I am the light of the world. Whoever follows me will not walk in darkness but will have the light of life (John 8:12, ESV).

- ♥ *Lion of the Tribe of Judah-* And one of the elders said to me, "Weep no more; behold, the Lion of the tribe of Judah, the Root of David, has conquered, so that he can open the scroll and its seven seals (Revelation 5:5, ESV).

- ♥ *Lord of all-* Therefore God has highly exalted him and bestowed on him the name that is above every name, so that at the name of Jesus every knee should bow, in heaven and on earth and under the earth, and every tongue confess that Jesus Christ is Lord, to the glory of God the Father (Philippians 2:9-11, ESV).

- ♥ *Wonderful Counselor, Mighty God, Everlasting Father, Prince of Peace-* For to us a child is born, to us a son is given, and the government will be on his shoulders and he will be called Wonderful Counselor, Mighty God, Everlasting Father, Prince of Peace (Isaiah 9:6, NIV).

♥ *Our Hope-* Paul, an apostle of Christ Jesus by command of God our Savior and of Christ Jesus our hope (1 Timothy 1:1, ESV).

♥ *Prophet-* Moses said, The Lord God will raise up for you a prophet like me from your brothers. You shall listen to him in whatever he tells you (Acts 3:22, Deuteronomy 18:18, Mark 6:4, ESV).

♥ *Redeemer-* For I know that my Redeemer lives and at the last he will stand upon the earth (Job 19:25, ESV).

♥ *Solid Rock-* as it is written behold, I am laying in Zion a stone of stumbling, and a rock of offense; and whoever believes in him will not be put to shame and all drank the same spiritual drink. For they drank from the spiritual Rock that followed them, and the Rock was Christ (Romans 9:33, 1 Corinthians 10:4, 2 Samuel 22:47, ESV).

♥ *Savior-* For unto you is born this day in the city of David a Savior, who is Christ the Lord. (Luke 2:11, Matthew 1:21, ESV).

♥ **Stronghold, fortress, refuge, and strength-** I love you, Lord, my strength. The Lord is my rock, my fortress, and my deliverer; my God is my rock, in whom I take refuge, my shield and the horn of my salvation, my stronghold (Psalm 18:1-2; NIV)

♥ *The Anointed One-* The Spirit of the Lord is upon me, because he has anointed me to proclaim good news to the poor. He has sent me to proclaim liberty to the captives and recovering of sight to the blind, to set at liberty those who are oppressed (Luke 4:18, ESV).

♥ *The Truth-* Jesus said to him, "I am the way, and **the truth,** and the life. No one comes to the Father except through me (John14:6, ESV).

- ♥ **The Door-** I am the door. If anyone enters by me, he will be saved and will go in and out and find pasture (John 10:9, ESV).

- ♥ **The Way-** Jesus said to him, "I am **the way**, and the truth, and the life. No one comes to the Father except through me (John14:6, ESV).

- ♥ **The True Vine-** I am the true vine, and my Father is the vinedresser. Every branch in me that does not bear fruit he takes away, and every branch that does bear fruit he prunes, that it may bear more fruit (John 15:1-2, ESV).

- ♥ **The One who holds the keys to shut and to open-** to the angel of the church in Philadelphia write: These are the words of him who is holy and true, who holds the key of David. What he opens no one can shut, and what he shuts no one can open (Revelation 3:7, Isaiah 22:22, NIV).

- ♥ **Victorious One-** To the one who is victorious, I will give the right to sit with me on my throne, just as I was victorious and sat down with my Father on his throne ([38]Revelation 3:21, NIV).

---

[38] Scripture quotations identified throughout this book in KJV (King James Version), NKJV (New King James Versions), NLT (New Living Translation Version), AMPC(Amplified Version Classic Edition),AMP, (Amplified Bible), ESV(English Standard Version), NIV(New International Version), and NASB (New American Standard Bible) and others indicated are from www.biblegateway.com

ATTRIBUTES OF THE
HOLY SPIRIT

CHAPTER 30

John 14:15-17- *If you love Me, keep My commandments and I will pray the Father, and He will give you another Helper, that He may abide with you forever. The Spirit of truth, whom the world cannot receive, because it neither sees Him nor knows Him; but you know Him, for He dwells with you and will be in you. I will not leave you orphans; I will come to you. (NKJV).*

The Old Testament speaks of the promise of the Holy Spirit, see Joel 2:29. John the Baptist confirms the promise in Matthew 3:11: *"I indeed baptize you with water unto repentance, but He who is coming after me is mightier than I, whose sandals I am not worthy to carry. He will baptize you with the **Holy Spirit and fire"*** (NJKV). This promise was fulfilled by Jesus Christ, see John chapters 14 through 17.

The actual baptism of the Holy Spirit and fire occurs in the beginning chapters of the book of Acts. I have intentionally included the attributes of the Holy Spirit in this book; we cannot pray without Him. There is nothing we can accomplish successfully as believers without the help of the Holy Spirit, and that includes our effectiveness in prayer.

In reviewing the roles and attributes of the Holy Spirit, it is evident that the Holy Spirit captures and addresses all areas of our lives based on His responsibilities to us. The Holy Spirit is the fullness of the

Trinity, assigned to live and work in us, through us and for us. That said, it is paramount that we foster relationship and collaborate with the Holy Spirit, because the promise of the Holy Spirit is not limited to an infilling but an actual and constant immersion in Him through fellowship. The Holy Spirit works greatly when invited and given liberty to operate.

When we engage with the Holy Spirit in prayer, He accordingly helps us stay on target, bringing us the needed breakthrough. I have learned to apply the attributes of the Holy Spirit when I pray. For example, when I am tired and when I need comfort, I pray, "Holy Spirit as Comforter, comfort me through this situation and strengthen and empower me to accomplish this task." I hope you can see how the attributes of the Holy Spirit blend with the Names of God and the attributes of Jesus Christ. Through this, as we pray, we see the union of the Trinity: God the Father, God the Son and God the Holy Spirit.

All of our prayers are addressed to God our Father; as you pray, pray with the Holy Spirit, and pray also in the Spirit. In the next chapter I will share about the benefits of praying in the language of the Holy Spirit also known as tongues or prayer language. For now, please see the following roles of the Holy Spirit, and purpose to connect with them during prayer and in your life.

- *Intercessor*- Romans 8:26-27: Likewise the Spirit helps us in our weakness. For we do not know what to pray for as we ought, but the Spirit himself intercedes for us with groanings too deep for words and he who searches hearts knows what the mind of the Spirit is, because the Spirit intercedes for the saints according to the will of God (ESV).

- *Anointing*-The Holy Spirit is the anointing. He is the Power of God- Luke 4:18-19: The Spirit of the Lord is upon Me, because He has anointed Me, to preach the gospel to the poor; He has sent Me to heal the brokenhearted, to proclaim liberty to the captives and recovery of sight to the blind, to set at liberty those who are oppressed; to proclaim the acceptable year of the Lord (ESV). 2 Corinthians 1:21-22: Now He who establishes us with you in Christ and has anointed us is God, who also has sealed us and given us the Spirit in our hearts as a guarantee (NKJV). The anointing is also the Oil of the Spirit.

- *Helper-* John 14:15-16: If you love Me, keep My commandments and I will pray the Father, and He will give you another Helper, that He may abide with you forever (NKJV).

- *Comforter-* John 14:16: And I will pray the Father, and he shall give you another Comforter, that he may abide with you forever (KJV).

- *Teacher-* John 14:26: But the Helper, the Holy Spirit, whom the Father will send in My name, He will teach you all things, and bring to your remembrance all things that I said to you (NKJV).

- *Helps recall previous Instructions-* John 14:26: But the Helper, the Holy Spirit, whom the Father will send in My name, He will teach you all things, and *bring to your remembrance all things that I said to you.* When we forget the instructions God has given us, the Holy Spirit is able to bring such to our recollection. I have experienced this a lot when I am praying or when I am reflecting on God. This is a great attribute of the Holy Spirit.

- *Advocate-True Witness-* John 15:26: But when the Helper comes, whom I shall send to you from the Father, the Spirit of truth who proceeds from the Father, He will testify of Me and you also will bear witness, because you have been with Me from the beginning (NKJV). The Holy Spirit as our advocate or lawyer representative, bears witness that we are children of God, He backs us up. Romans 8:16: The Spirit himself bears witness with our spirit that we are children of God.

- *Guidance -Guide in truth-* John 16:13: However, when He, the Spirit of truth, has come, He will guide you into all truth; for He will not speak on His own authority, but whatever He hears He will speak; and He will tell you things to come (NKJV).

- *Convict of Sin-* John 16:7: The Helper will not come to you; but if I depart, I will send Him to you and when He has come, He will convict the world of sin, and of righteousness, and of judgment of sin, because they do not believe in Me (NKJV).

- *Revelator and Prophet-* John 16:13-15: However, when He, the Spirit of truth, has come, He will guide you into all truth; for He will not speak on His own authority, but whatever He hears He will speak; and He will tell you things to come. He will glorify Me, for He will take of what is Mine and declare it to you. All things that the Father has are Mine. Therefore I said that He will take of Mine and declare it to you. The Holy Spirit revealer of God's secrets, minds, will concerning us and shows us things to come.

- *Sanctifier-* Galatians 5:16-18: This I say then, walk in the Spirit, and ye shall not fulfil the lust of the flesh. For the flesh lusteth against the Spirit, and the Spirit against the flesh: and these are contrary the one to the other: so that ye cannot do the things that ye would but if ye be led of the Spirit, ye are not under the law (KJV).

- *Strengthens and Empowers-* Romans 8:11: If the Spirit of him who raised Jesus from the dead dwells in you, he who raised Christ Jesus from the dead will also give life to your mortal bodies through his Spirit who dwells in you (ESV). Zechariah 4:6: Then he answered and spake unto me, saying, This is the word of the Lord unto Zerubbabel, saying, Not by might, nor by power, but by my spirit, saith the Lord of hosts (KJV).

- *Power for Evangelist Work-* Acts 1:8: But you shall receive power when the Holy Spirit has come upon you; and you shall be witnesses to

Me in Jerusalem, and in all Judea and Samaria, and to the end of the earth (NKJV). The Holy Spirit strengthens us to accomplish God's work, gives us boldness and courage. The Holy Spirit gives us power to witness, heal and deliver see Acts 4:31: and when they had prayed, the place where they were assembled together was shaken; and they were all filled with the Holy Spirit, and they spoke the word of God with boldness (NJKV).

- *Bears Fruit-* Galatians 5:22-23: But the fruit of the Spirit is love, joy, peace, patience, kindness, goodness, faithfulness, gentleness, self-control; against such things there is no law (ESV).

- *Fills Us-* Ephesians 5:18-19: And do not be drunk with wine, in which is dissipation; but be filled with the Spirit, speaking to one another in psalms and hymns and spiritual songs, singing and making melody in your heart to the Lord, He fills us (NKJV). To be filled with the Spirit means we are fully immersed in Him, have surrendered our lives to Him, acknowledging that He owns us and has the right to lead us. When we are fully yielded and walking in obedience to His will, then He has full control and fills us with Himself.

- *Equipper-* The Holy Spirit gives us the tools to be successful in our callings and destinies.

1Corinthians 12:4-11: There are diversities of gifts, but the same Spirit. There are differences of ministries, but the same Lord. And there are diversities of activities, but it is the same God who works all in all. But the manifestation of the Spirit is given to each one for the profit of all :for to one is given the word of wisdom through the Spirit, to another the word of knowledge through the same Spirit, to another faith by the same Spirit, to another gifts of healings by the same Spirit, to another the working of miracles, to another prophecy, to another discerning of spirits, to another different kinds of tongues, to another the interpretation of tongues. But one and the same Spirit works all these things, distributing to each one individually as He wills (NKJV).

- *Refreshes and Renews-* Isaiah 28:11-12: For with stammering lips and another tongue will speak to this people, To whom He said, "This is the rest with which you may cause the weary to rest, and, "This is the refreshing"; yet they would not hear (NKJV). *Isaiah 44:3:* For I will pour out water on the thirsty land And streams on the dry ground; I will pour out My Spirit on your offspring And My blessing on your descendants (ESV).

- *Rivers of Living Water-* John 7:37-39: Now on the last day, the great day of the feast, Jesus stood and cried out, saying, "If anyone is thirsty, let him come to Me and drink. "He who believes in Me, as the Scripture said, 'From his innermost being will flow rivers of living water.'" But this He spoke of the Spirit, whom those who believed in Him were to receive; for the Spirit was not yet given, because Jesus was not yet glorified (ESV). John 4:14: but whoever drinks of the water that I will give him shall never thirst; but the water that I will give him will become in him a well of water springing up to eternal life (ESV).

- *Mighty Rushing Wind-* Act 2:1-4: When the Day of Pentecost had fully come, they were all [a]with one accord in one place and suddenly there came a sound from heaven, as of a rushing mighty wind, and it filled the whole house where they were sitting. Then there appeared to them divided tongues, as of fire, and one sat upon each of them and they were all filled with the Holy Spirit and began to speak with other tongues, as the Spirit gave them utterance ([39]NKJV).

---

[39] Scripture quotations identified throughout this book in KJV (King James Version), NKJV (New King James Versions), NLT (New Living Translation Version), AMPC(Amplified Version Classic Edition),AMP, (Amplified Bible), ESV(English Standard Version), NIV(New International Version), and NASB (New American Standard Bible) and others indicated are from www.biblegateway.com

The Rain of the Spirit- God's Spirit Poured

And it shall come to pass in the last days, says God, that I will pour out of My Spirit on all flesh; your sons and your daughters shall prophesy, your young men shall see visions, your old men shall dream dreams and on My menservants and on My maidservants, I will pour out My Spirit in those days; and they shall prophesy. I will show wonders in heaven above and signs in the earth beneath: blood and fire and vapor of smoke. The sun shall be turned into darkness and the moon into blood, before the coming of the great and awesome day of the Lord and it shall come to pass that whoever calls on the name of the Lord Shall be saved. ([40]Acts4:17-21; NKJV).

---

[40] Scripture quotations identified throughout this book in KJV (King James Version), NKJV (New King James Versions), NLT (New Living Translation Version), AMPC(Amplified Version Classic Edition),AMP, (Amplified Bible), ESV(English Standard Version), NIV(New International Version), and NASB (New American Standard Bible) and others indicated are from www.biblegateway.com

BENEFITS OF PRAYING IN TONGUES

When you are baptized in the Holy Spirit you are often given the gift of praying in tongues. We first see evidence of this gift in Acts 2:1-4: *"When the day of Pentecost came, they were all together in one place. Suddenly a sound like the blowing of a violent wind came from heaven and filled the whole house where they were sitting. They saw what seemed to be tongues of fire that separated and came to rest on each of them. All of them were filled with the Holy Spirit and began to speak in other tongues[a] as the Spirit enabled them"* (NIV). The in-filling or baptism of the Holy Spirit is ongoing as evidenced by the multiple occasions that the disciples were filled with the Holy Spirit. See Acts 4:31: *"And when they had prayed, the place where they were assembled together was shaken; and they were all filled with the Holy Spirit, and they spoke the word of God with boldness"* (NKJV); and Acts 10: 44-46: *"While Peter was still speaking these words, the Holy Spirit came on all who heard the message. The circumcised believers who had come with Peter were astonished that the gift of the Holy Spirit had been poured out even on Gentiles. For they heard them speaking in tongues and praising God"* (NIV).

The spiritual gift of tongues is also in outlined 1 Corinthians 12:10: *"To another the working of miracles; to another prophecy; to another discerning of spirits; to another diverse kinds of tongues; to another the interpretation of tongues" (KJV).* Tongues as many born again Christians know it, is the language of heaven or the language of the Holy Spirit. It may also be referred to as the prayer language or pray in the Spirit. The Bible encourages us to pray all types of prayers in the Spirit as stated in Ephesians 6:17-18: *"And take the helmet of salvation, and the sword of the Spirit, which is the word of God; praying always with all prayer and supplication in the Spirit, being watchful to this end with all perseverance and supplication for all the saints"* (NKJV).

I have included this topic in this book because praying in the Spirit and with the Holy Spirit are critical tools in all types of prayer, including utilizing the Names of God as you pray. It is appropriate to include the Holy Spirit in any topic related to prayer. As you apply the Names and attributes of the Trinity in your prayers, incorporate praying in tongues; below are the benefits of praying in tongues:

- Praying in tongues aligns you with Holy Spirit, resulting in empowerment to pray accurately the will of God concerning your need. Romans 8:27: *Now He who searches the hearts knows what the mind of the Spirit is, because He makes intercession for the saints according to the will of God (NKJV).*

- Praying in tongues allows for direct communication with God. 1 Corinthians 14:2: *For he who speaks in a tongue does not speak to men but to God, for no one understands him; however, in the spirit he speaks mysteries (NKJV).*

- Praying in tongues is a spiritual gift for communication with God in private devotion or worship. 1 Corinthians 14:15: *What is the conclusion then? I will pray with the spirit, and I will also pray with the understanding. I will sing with the spirit, and I will also sing with the understanding ([41]NKJV).*

---

[41] Scripture quotations identified throughout this book in KJV (King James Version), NKJV (New King James Versions), NLT (New Living Translation Version), AMPC(Amplified Version Classic Edition),AMP, (Amplified Bible), ESV(English Standard Version), NIV(New International Version), and NASB (New American Standard Bible) and others indicated are from www.biblegateway.com

- Praying in tongues is a means by which the Holy Spirit intercedes through us and for us. Romans 8:26: *Likewise, the Spirit also helps in our weaknesses. For we do not know what we should pray for as we ought, but the Spirit Himself makes intercession for us with groanings which cannot be uttered* [42]*(NKJV).*

- Praying in tongues edifies, empowers, stirs up our faith and strengthens us. Praying in tongues plays a big role in edifying the church fellowship or gathering. 1 Corinthians 14:4: *He who speaks in a tongue edifies himself, but he who prophesies edifies the church (NKJV).* Also see Jude 1:20 *But you, beloved, building yourselves up on your most holy faith, praying in the Holy Spirit* (NKJV).

- Praying in tongues is a means by which we obtain new revelation from God. 1 Corinthians 2:9-12: *But as it is written: "Eye has not seen, nor ear heard, Nor have entered into the heart of man the things which God has prepared for those who love Him." But God has revealed them to us through His Spirit. For the Spirit searches all things, yes, the deep things of God. For what man knows the things of a man except the spirit of the man which is in him? Even so no one knows the things of God except the Spirit of God. Now we have received, not the spirit of the world, but the Spirit who is from God, that we might know the things that have been freely given to us by God (NKJV).*

- Praying in tongues refreshes and renews us; it helps us overcome heaviness and weariness of the soul. Isaiah 28:11-18: *For with stammering lips and another tongue He will speak to this people, To whom He said, "This is the rest with which you may cause the weary to rest," and, "This is the refreshing," Yet they would not hear (NKJV).*

---

[42] Scripture quotations identified throughout this book in KJV (King James Version), NKJV (New King James Versions), NLT (New Living Translation Version), AMPC(Amplified Version Classic Edition),AMP, (Amplified Bible), ESV(English Standard Version), NIV(New International Version), and NASB (New American Standard Bible) and others indicated are from www.biblegateway.com

- By praying in tongues, we proclaim the mysteries of God. 1 Corinthians 14:2: *For he who speaks in a tongue does not speak to men but to God, for no one understands him; however, in the spirit he speaks mysteries (NKJV).*

- Praying in tongues fuels, stirs up and advances our spiritual gifts. This is one of the ways spiritual gifts can be developed and accelerated. 2 Timothy 1:6 -7: *Therefore, I remind you to stir up the gift of God which is in you through the laying on of my hands. For God has not given us a spirit of fear, but of power and of love and of a sound mind (NKJV).*

- Praying tongues creates courage and boldness, warding off fear. Acts 4:23-31: *And being let go, they went to their own companions and reported all that the chief priests and elders had said to them. So when they heard that, they raised their voice to God with one accord and said: "Lord, You are God, who made heaven and earth and the sea, and all that is in them, who by the mouth of Your servant David have said: 'Why did the nations rage, and the people plot vain things? The kings of the earth took their stand and the rulers were gathered together. Against the Lord and against His Christ.' For truly against Your holy Servant Jesus, whom You anointed, both Herod and Pontius Pilate, with the Gentiles and the people of Israel, were gathered together to do whatever Your hand and Your purpose determined before to be done. Now, Lord, look on their threats, and grant to Your servants that with all boldness they may speak Your word, by stretching out Your hand to heal, and that signs and wonders may be done through the name of Your holy Servant Jesus. And when they had prayed, the place where they were assembled together was shaken; and they <u>were all filled with the Holy Spirit, and they spoke the word of God with boldness</u> (NKJV).*

I end this book with a word of encouragement to you- that as you pray, know that your prayers are being heard and that God will respond. Pray more in tongues. Remember that you have the support of both Jesus Christ and the Holy Spirit interceding for you; as well as Angels whom God has assigned to act on His word concerning you. *God is not a man, that he should lie, nor a human being, that he should change his mind. Has he said, and will he not do it? Or has he spoken, and will he not make it happen;* (Numbers 23:19, NET). The Lord is not slow in keeping his promise, as some understand slowness. With the Lord a day is like a thousand years, and a thousand years are like a day. God answers prayers!

I pray that the Spirit of the Lord may rest upon you. The Spirit of wisdom and understanding, The Spirit of counsel and might, The Spirit of knowledge and The Spirit of the fear of the Lord (Isaiah 11:2, NKJV).

Now unto Him that is able to keep you from falling, and to present you faultless before the presence of His glory with exceeding joy; to the only wise God our Saviour, be glory and majesty, dominion, and power. Unto the King eternal, immortal, invisible, be honor and glory for ever and ever ([43]Jude 24,25, NKJV; KJV) Amen.

---

[43] Scripture quotations identified throughout this book in KJV (King James Version), NKJV (New King James Versions), NLT (New Living Translation Version), AMPC(Amplified Version Classic Edition),AMP, (Amplified Bible), ESV(English Standard Version), NIV(New International Version), and NASB (New American Standard Bible) and others indicated are from www.biblegateway.com

THE PRAYER OF SALVATION AND THE BAPTISM OF THE HOLY SPIRIT

Jesus Christ is the Key through whom we get to access God. We cannot know God without knowing Jesus. Jesus shares this assurance in John 14:6 NIV, "**I am the way, the truth, and the life. No one can come to the Father except through Me**". Accepting Jesus Christ as your Lord and Savior will grant you access to start enjoying the fullness of God.

Jesus died for our redemption, deliverance and healing, as stated in the book of Isaiah, *"Jesus was wounded for our transgressions, He was bruised for our iniquities; the chastisement for our peace was upon Him, and by His stripes we are healed", (Isaiah 53:5 NKJV)*. If you want to invite Jesus into your life, pray the prayer below out loud:

Dear God, I come to You. I accept your Son Jesus Christ as my Lord and Savior. I believe that Jesus died and rose again for my sins, so that I may receive salvation. I therefore repent of my sins, transgressions and iniquities and ask for Your forgiveness. I renounce sin and all forms of wickedness. I renounce all gods that I have served, vowed to, submitted to, or ever made sacrifices to them. Lord Jesus, now come into my life and into everything that concerns me. Come in, Lord Jesus, and be Lord over my life and align me to the path and plan you have for me. In the name of Jesus Christ, I pray. Amen.

Now invite the Holy Spirit who will help, teach, and guide in this new life. You can pray: *Holy Spirit, I now welcome You. Come to reside in me and take over every aspect of my life. I submit to You Holy Spirit; guide me in knowledge, wisdom, revelation, discernment, and counsel so that I may walk and accomplish the plan God has for me. Holy Spirit fill me with your gifts that I may experience the fullness of God in this new life, in the name of Jesus I pray. Amen!*

If you have sincerely prayed the prayer above, with all your heart, then welcome to God's family, you are a now a child of God who is clothed in righteousness. Christ is now living in you and His fullness is operating through the Holy Spirit. This my prayer for you:

In the Mighty Name of Jesus, and by the blood of the Lamb, I command you to be delivered from any bondage of Satan. I rebuke, flush out, and expel any demonic occupant in your life, your bloodline, and your body. I loose you from every bondage of Satan. You are now set free by the blood of the Lamb. Receive your healing. Receive your deliverance.

I command your mind to be restored, in the Mighty Name of Jesus. Receive restoration and restitution. I command permanency of the good things God has started in you. I decree your Fruitfulness, Multiplication, Sustainability, and Longevity in everything God has for you, according to His perfect will and plan, in the Mighty Name of Jesus! Amen! And Amen!

Next please purchase a Bible that you can write notes in; a version that you can easily understand, such as NLT, NJKV or ESV translations. Start by reading the Gospel of John; then read the book of Proverbs, then the New Testament from Matthew to Revelation. Try reading a chapter in the morning and one at night before bedtime; followed by prayer. Do this regularly. Also find a Spirit-filled church that you can attend. Let the pastor know that you recently accepted Jesus as your Savior; ask them to baptize you by immersion in water. Then ask the pastor to direct you on how to be discipled. The Holy Spirit will also teach and disciple you; just ask Him. Welcome to God's Kingdom!

ABOUT THE AUTHOR

Pauline Adongo is a missionary and itinerant minister whose passion is to equip and prepare the body of Christ. Her mandate is to harvest souls and disciple believers globally. Through preaching the gospel billions will receive salvation, deliverance, healing, and restoration. Pauline's goal is to see each believer mature and come to enjoy their fullness in Christ Jesus. She is a global missionary and travels locally and internationally to accomplish the mission God has assigned her. Pauline has authored other books that are available on her website; www.paulineadongo.com. She is the founder and president of The Ministry of Jesus Christ International Inc. Harvest- Equip-Disciple and Ignite Nations! Follow Pauline on social media.

Printed in the United States
By Bookmasters